# Shit You Need To Do Before You Die

## From Bucket List to Burial Plans

SHELLI NETKO

# Shit You Need To Do Before You Die: From Bucket List To Burial
## Workbook Edition




Published by Heart to Heart Collective
Scottsdale, Arizona

Printed in the United States of America

For more resources, visit: shellinetko.com


## Disclaimer (a.k.a. Don't Sue Me):

I'm not an attorney, accountant, healthcare provider, or funeral planner—nor do I play one on TV. Everything in this book was gathered from Google, AI, and a few too-honest life lessons. This is your playbook, not your legal paperwork. Use it to get your shit together—then check with a pro to see what fits your real-life (and death) situation.

# *Dedicated to...*

*To my sister —*
*Who became the parent our parents needed.*
*You saw what was coming before anyone else did,*
*and you carried the weight of their care*
*with grace, strength, and love that went far beyond duty.*
*You gave them comfort, dignity, and peace at a time*
*when they needed it most.*

**To Joe —**
*Who never hesitated, never turned away.*
*In every season of need, your answer was always yes.*
*Your quiet generosity and unwavering heart proved*
*that true goodness isn't measured by recognition,*
*but by the lives quietly lifted up along the way.*

**To my late husband and partner in crime for 22 years —**
*When you died, the world became quiet.*
*Yet in the silence, I could still hear you—*
*in your love, your lessons,*
*and the inspiration you left behind.*

*You showed me how to live in love*
*and to reach for more every single day.*
*Your fingerprints are on these pages,*
*a reminder of what life and loss can teach us—*
*and of the importance of leaving the Wi-Fi password*
*before you take that final trip to heaven.*

# Table of contents

# PREFACE

Dying is a funny thing, isn't it?

Okay, no—it's not funny. At all. It's terrifying, awkward, and right up there with tax audits and swimsuit shopping in bad lighting. Most of us would rather wrestle an angry raccoon than talk about death. We'll joke about "living to 100" or pretend we're too busy to deal with it, but the truth is, unless you've discovered the fountain of youth (and haven't told the rest of us), you're not getting out of this alive.

At last count, there were about 8.1 billion people walking around this planet. And guess what? Every single one of them has an expiration date. Some are just a lot closer than they'd like to admit.

But here's the crazy thing: we'll spend hours scrolling Airbnbs for a weekend getaway, or researching where to get the best tacos in town, yet we'll avoid planning for the one thing that's guaranteed to happen. (Seriously—why do we know where our next vacation is but not who gets Grandma's jewelry box or who will be the guardian of our children?)

**Why?** **Because most of us fall into one of two camps:**

**The Planners** – Those mystical creatures who already have their will, passwords, and funeral playlist neatly filed in color-coded binders. They're rare—like people who actually floss twice a day or return shopping carts in the rain.

 **The Procrastinators** – The rest of us. Too young, too busy, too overwhelmed, or too freaked out. We tell ourselves there's time, or that someone else will handle it "when the time comes." (Newsflash: that "someone else" is usually your exhausted family, cursing your name while digging through junk drawers for your will—or worse, your Facebook login so they can tell your friends you can't make it to happy hour.

The funny thing is, refusing to plan doesn't make death go away. It just makes the aftermath messier than a toddler with a Sharpie. Without a plan, your loved ones are stuck with mountains of red tape, endless decisions, and bills they didn't sign up for. With a plan, you get to leave behind something better than a disaster: you leave peace, clarity, and maybe even a laugh or two if you throw in your weird funeral requests.

That's where this book comes in. Think of it as your "Death Prep Starter Kit." Part diary, part instruction manual, part "holy shit, I should've done this years ago." It's easy to follow, doesn't require a law degree, and won't make your eyes glaze over like most estate-planning seminars. You'll find checklists, prompts, and space to scribble down the important stuff (like where you hid the good wine, who gets the dog, or who should never, under any circumstances, give a speech at your funeral).

By the end, you'll have your shit together in a way that actually matters. Not just "I color-coded my pantry" kind of together. I mean legacy-level together. The kind that saves your family from headaches, heartache, and the "why didn't they plan for this?" rant that nobody wants to be remembered for.

So here's the deal: it's not too late. You're alive, you're reading this, and that means you've got time. Time to quit pretending you're immortal and start doing the *Shit You Need To Do Before You Die.*

Grab a pen. Pour a drink. Write down the Wi-Fi password. And let's make you the ultimate planner.

# Master Index

Before you get started, it helps to have a preview of what you'll be gathering and working on. This is the quick-glance guide to all you where important documents, accounts, and "must-knows" live. Think of it as your family's treasure map (without the pirate's booty.)

Now don't let any of this scare you. We'll cover all of it in so much detail you'll feel like a boss when we're done.

### Personal Information

- Full name, date of birth
- Social Security number
- Marriage/divorce certificates
- Children & next of kin info
- Religious preferences
- Emergency contacts

### Identification Documents

- Birth certificate
- Passport(s)
- Driver's license / state ID
- Military records (if applicable)

### Health & Medical

- Advance directive / living will
- Healthcare proxy / medical POA
- Do Not Resuscitate (DNR) / POLST
- Organ donor registration
- Medical history & records
- Medications, allergies, insurance cards

### Financial Accounts

- Bank accounts (checking, savings, credit unions)
- Investments (brokerage, stocks, bonds)
- Retirement accounts (401k, IRA, Roth, SEP, etc.)
- **Retirement plans & pensions**
- Crypto wallets

### Insurance

- Life insurance policies
- Health insurance policies
- Auto / home / renter's insurance
- Professional / liability insurance

### Property & Assets

- Real estate (deeds, mortgages, titles)
- Vehicles (cars, boats, RVs, motorcycles)

- Personal property of value (jewelry, collections, heirlooms)
- Safe deposit box information

## Employment & Business

- Employer information (HR contact, benefits, payroll)
- Professional licenses/certifications
- Business ownership documents
- Partnerships / contracts

## Debts & Liabilities

- Mortgages
- Car loans
- Student loans
- Credit cards
- Other personal loans / lines of credit

## Digital Estate

- Social media logins
- Email accounts
- Cloud storage (Google Drive, iCloud, Dropbox)
- Domains, websites, online businesses
- Subscriptions (streaming, gym, Amazon, Peloton, etc.)

## Memberships & Organizations

- Professional associations

- Alumni groups

- Clubs / community memberships Volunteer organizations

- Unions

## Legal Documents

- Will & trust

- Power of attorney (financial & medical)

- Beneficiary designations

- Guardianship papers

## Funeral & Final Plans

- Burial/cremation choice

- Service preferences (funeral, memorial, celebration of life)

- People to notify

- Special requests (music, readings, location)

## Legacy & Memories

- Letters to loved ones

- Journals, audio/video messages

- Recipes, traditions

- Memory boxes or keepsakes

# CHAPTER 1

# Bucket List Basics

## *(a.k.a. Don't Make It a F*ck-It List)*

> *Tick-tock, baby.*
> *You can't fill your bucket*
> *list once you kick it.*

"Why make a bucket list? Because if you don't, life will happily bury you under laundry, emails, and dentist appointments until one day you wake up and realize... oh shit, I ran out of tomorrows." We've all heard about bucket lists, but let's be real — most people talk about them the way they talk about going to the gym: with good intentions and little follow-through. The term itself comes from "kick the bucket," which is a charming way of saying "die." So your bucket list is basically all the stuff you want to do before you *kick it.*

Here's the catch: too many people just toss ideas around over cocktails — "I should totally put that on my bucket list!" — but never actually write them down. And you know what happens then? Your shiny bucket list quietly morphs into a "f*ck-it list" — something you'll "get to later" until later turns into never, and then... well, you actually kick the bucket. Then you are buried or cremated along with all your broken promises and empty dreams.

Don't let that be your story. Write the damn list. Then start living it.

## Why the Bucket List Actually Matters (and Why It's Not Just BS)

Listen, this isn't about crafting a cute Instagram caption or low key bragging at brunch. A bucket list is about living on purpose. It's about shaking yourself out of autopilot and asking, "If fear, money, or time weren't holding me hostage, what would I actually want to do with this one wild life?"

Without a list, life turns into Groundhog Day: work, bills, dishes, repeat. Before you know it, ten years have evaporated and you still haven't written the book, taken the trip, or said the thing you swore you'd say "someday."

A bucket list is your personal permission slip. It says: *stop waiting for someday — today is the day.*

And here's the real secret: once you cross off one thing, you create momentum. You finally sign up for that pottery class, and suddenly your brain goes, "Wait... I can actually do this stuff." Before long, you're skydiving, planning that Italy trip, or maybe even starting the side hustle you've been daydreaming about since you can remember.

## Hack Your List Like a Pro

Forget the Pinterest-perfect version of sitting down with a leather journal and a glass of wine to dream up your list. Real life doesn't work that way. Busy people nap, scroll, and binge Netflix with their spare 20 minutes. So instead, catch your ideas on the fly.

Use your phone apps — Notes, Reminders, whatever. Because those brilliant "I want to do THAT!" moments usually strike when you're in the shower, stuck in traffic, or pretending to listen during a Zoom call. Those sparks are gold. Capture them before they vanish.

Before you begin, understand that your list should look nothing like anyone else's. Because what lights you up might bore someone else to tears. If you geek out on history, great — put "tour every Civil War battlefield" on there. If you'd rather stick a fork in your eye than go to a museum, skip it. If your dream is couch-napping every Sunday guilt-free, guess what? Put it on the list.

The whole point of a bucket list isn't to impress anyone. It's not about creating Instagram-worthy moments or building a highlight reel of your life. Your list is meant to be your heartbeat (a racing one.) It should make you feel alive — not serve as content for strangers online. That means it won't look like your spouse's, friend's, or your sister's. And it shouldn't.

If your best friend is dying to trek up Machu Picchu but you'd rather sip wine in Tuscany, then Peru doesn't belong on your list. If your spouse dreams of running a marathon but you'd rather run a bubble bath, own it. And if your cousin can't wait to leap off bridges with a bungee cord while you get queasy on a step stool, don't even bother pretending. This is your list, not theirs. Borrowing other people's dreams is a waste of the limited time you've got here, and nobody likes a phony.

Some items will be epic. Seeing the Northern Lights, climbing a mountain, finishing that book, or traveling across Europe. Others will be quiet but just as sacred: finally sitting down at the piano you've had for years, planting sunflowers in the backyard, baking Grandma's pie recipe from scratch, or just sitting on your porch to watch a thunderstorm roll in with someone you love.

Sometimes it's the little things... example: I've had "take a one-horse open sleigh ride in the snow" on my list for as long as I can remember. It might seem silly to you, and I'm okay with that. Big or small, if it stirs something in you, it belongs on the list.

That's the rule of thumb. If you've ever caught yourself thinking, *"I want to do that someday,"* it's a bucket list item. Period. No editing, no justifying, no dismissing as "too small" or "too silly." Write it down.

Your list is a permission slip to stop waiting for someday. Later is a myth. The laundry, the bills, the deadlines — they'll always be there. But your chances won't. Life doesn't politely hand you free time for your dreams. You make it. You Take it. You create it. You claim it.

So start now. Write the book. Take the trip. Nap without guilt. Order dessert first. Book the country swing class. Call the person. Do the thing. Because at the end of it all, a bucket list isn't really about what you'll do before you die.

It's about how fully you'll live while you're here.

| DO | DON'T |
|---|---|
| ✓ Keep ideas flowing. | ✗ Judge your ideas ("too expensive, too crazy, too late"). |
| ✓ Dream big and small. | ✗ Edit yourself before you've even started. |
| ✓ Let your future self get excited. | ✗ Let the inner naysayer run the show. |

## The Top 16 – America's Bucket List

Curious what the rest of the country is dreaming about? Researchers at Today. YouGov.com pulled together what they call America's ultimate bucket list — and let's just say it's a mix of inspiring, predictable, and a little underwhelming. (Spoiler: the number one goal wasn't "see the world" or "write a book"... it was not exactly sexy, but it was honest.)

# (Top 16)



1 Get healthier/lose weight

2 Travel to an exotic location

3 Achieve a wealth goal (pay off debt, save big)

4 See a natural wonder

5 Change someone's life for the better

6 Own a home

7 Get married

8 Learn a new language

9 Have children

10 Start a business

11 Meet a celebrity

12 Do an extreme sport (skydiving, bungee jumping, etc.)

13 Attend a big music festival

14 Write a novel

15 Complete a physical feat (marathon, climb a mountain, etc.)

16 Invent something

*Take this list as inspiration, not gospel. Your bucket list should look like you, not America.*

# Chapter Summary – Bucket List

At the end of the day, your bucket list comes down to a few simple truths. Start with a little soul searching and get honest about what you really want. Stop putting it off — procrastination is the graveyard of dreams. Use whatever tools you've got, even if that just means jotting ideas into your phone when inspiration strikes — while on a walk, at the symphony or during the season finale of your current binge.

Make sure your list looks like you and nobody else. Don't edit or judge your dreams before they've had a chance to live on paper. Stay open, stay positive, and don't let your inner critic shut it all down. And most importantly? Start now. Not "someday," not "later," not "when life finally slows down." Today is more than enough.

## Mini Reflective Exercise

Grab a notebook (or your phone if you're a notes-app junkie like me. Currently holding the world record with 1,851 phone notes.) Answer these, fast and unfiltered—no overthinking, no "but how," no excuses:

1. If tomorrow was your last day, what's the one thing you'd regret not doing?

_______________________________________________

_______________________________________________

_______________________________________________

2. What's something you've secretly wanted to try but never admitted out loud?

_______________________________________________

_______________________________________________

3. Name three small joys (not big, Instagram-worthy goals—just simple, human joys) you'd love to experience in the next 12 months.

_______________________________________________

_______________________________________________

_______________________________________________

Write them down. Don't edit, don't judge. This is your starting line.

_______________________________________________

_______________________________________________

_______________________________________________

"Dreams don't plan themselves. Use this page to map out what's next—adventures, experiences, and the crew you want with you. Because the best ideas are the ones you actually write down."

# CHAPTER 2

# GETTING YOUR Shit TOGETHER

*I regret getting organized. -- Said no one, ever.*

## *(a.k.a. The Personal Data Chapter)*

Here's the cold truth: you can have the sexiest bucket list in the world — sunsets in Santorini, bestselling novels, skydives swimming with sharks — but if you haven't wrangled the basics of your personal information, you're leaving behind a messy, expensive, stress-fueled scavenger hunt for the people who love you. And nothing kills the vibe faster than your family pawing through old tax returns and half-lit Christmas decorations while trying to find your Social Security card — all while simultaneously debating casket colors and floral arrangements.

It's not exactly the legacy you imagined, right? But that's what happens when your "life admin" is a mystery. Let's be real — your personal data and important documents aren't extras or "I'll get to it someday" tasks. They're the operating system of your life. When they're missing, things crash. Bills don't get paid. Insurance claims disappear into the bureaucratic abyss. Hospitals stall on treatment because no one knows what meds you're on. The government shows up with its clipboard and cold efficiency and when the government steps in, nobody wins).

And the people left behind? They're exhausted, grieving, and suddenly arguing about who was "supposed to" know where your will, passwords, or retirement info is. Every minute they spend hunting through boxes or waiting on hold with customer service is a minute they could have spent remembering you — not resenting the chaos you left behind.

Getting your paperwork together isn't morbid. It's mercy. It's the kindest thing you can do for the people you love. Because someday, when they're sitting around swapping stories about you, wouldn't you rather they be laughing about your karaoke skills than fighting over who gets stuck calling the IRS?

Sound dramatic? Try this on for size:

- You're unconscious in a hospital bed. No one knows your allergies or meds. Cue panic.

- You die without a will. Suddenly your least favorite in-law is weighing in on who gets your stuff.

- Your life insurance policy? Lost in a shoebox under expired Christmas lights. No one can find it.

That's not "planning." That's chaos. And it's why you need to get your shit together now.

## This Isn't Morbid. It's Kindness.

Getting organized isn't about control-freak energy. It's about being kind to the people who will have to pick up the pieces. It says: I care enough not to leave you knee-deep in paperwork, fighting over my Stanley collection.

Because here's a fact: even the sweetest families can turn into WWE wrestlers when death, money, and grief collide. Do you want your people sobbing together over your memory, or screaming at each other about who gets Grandma's pie recipe? Exactly.

# Quick Family Drama Prevention

Let's be real: nothing unleashes the drama like death. Here are a few crowd favorites you can prevent:

### The Facebook Feud

Cousin Tina announces your death online before your kids even knew. (Solution: a very clear emergency contact list.)

### The Jewelry Brawl

Sisters ready to rumble over Grandma's bling while Uncle Bob raids your liquor cabinet. (Solution: will + beneficiaries.)

### The Mystery Beneficiary

One of your exes shows up waving a bar napkin you once signed after three margaritas. (Solution: actual legal paperwork.)

### The Credit Card Surprise

Your spouse discovers six secret cards while bills keep rolling in. (Solution: account list, all of them.)

### The Netflix Meltdown

No one knows the password and now your kids can't binge their shows. (Solution: digital logins doc.)

**Moral of the story:** Organized = peace. Unorganized = reality TV family meltdown.

# What Counts as "Personal Information"?

Basically anything you've ever scribbled on a form, re-entered into an i-Pad at the doctor's office 47 times, or forgotten in a password manager. Start with:

- Date of birth  __________________________________________

- Emergency contacts  ______________________________

  ____________________________________________________

- Relationship status + spouse's info  ________________

  ____________________________________________________

- Your Contact details (phone, email, address, carrier pigeon
  if that's your thing)

  ____________________________________________________

  ____________________________________________________

  ____________________________________________________

  ____________________________________________________

- Religious preference  _____________________________

- Social Security number  ___________________________

- Health record highlights (chronic illnesses, surgeries, etc.)

  ____________________________________________________

  ____________________________________________________

- Medications, allergies, donor status  ______________

  ____________________________________________________

- People you *don't* want contacted (yes, that's a thing)

  ____________________________________________________

  ____________________________________________________

  ____________________________________________________

Think of this like your "All About Me" cheat sheet — the ultimate CliffsNotes of your life. If you were lost in the woods, this is what they'd hand the cops so they'd know who to look for (and which embarrassing nickname to avoid broadcasting over the radio). If you were unconscious in the ER, this is what the doctors would need before they start jabbing you with needles, guessing at your blood type, or calling your ex because they're still listed as your emergency contact from 2009.

And if you passed away? This is the map your family would cling to in the chaos — the one that keeps them from completely losing it while the world feels upside down. It tells them where the important things are: your bank accounts, your insurance info, your passwords, your wishes. It's the difference between calm clarity and frantic confusion. Between "We've got this" and "Wait—did anyone check the attic?"

Without it, even the most functional families can turn into a full-blown scavenger hunt gone wrong — picture siblings tearing through file cabinets like contestants on a sad reality show called *Who Finds the Will First? But with it*, you give your loved ones the gift of direction. They won't have to guess, argue, or call a psychic to figure out what you would've wanted. They'll just know.

So yes — this cheat sheet might look boring now, but someday it'll be the single most valuable document in your home. It's the blueprint that says, "Here's who I am, here's what matters, and here's how to keep things from falling apart."

## The Scavenger Hunt Nobody Wants

Here's the a nightmare scenario: you die, and your family spends weeks digging through closets, drawers, and bins in the attic like contestants on Storage Wars. Nobody wins.

Do the work now. Put it in one place. Because grief + paperwork is a no win situation.

## Documents That Matter

Let's be real — these are not sexy documents. Nobody frames their birth certificate or gets misty-eyed over a notarized will. But when life takes a hard left turn — an accident, illness, or the big finale — these are the papers that decide everything. Your birth certificate, Social Security card, passport, will or trust, living will, advance directive, and insurance policies aren't just paperwork; they're the proof, the plan, and the protection that holds your life together when everything else falls apart. Without them, your family is left guessing — calling banks, hunting for policies, and arguing over what you "probably wanted." With them, everything becomes clearer. Bills get paid. Benefits get released. Decisions get honored.

It's not fun, but neither is chaos, and this is how you avoid it. Gather them. Label them. Put them somewhere obvious. Because one day, these simple pages will mean everything to the people you love.

### Mini Homework Prompt:

Right now, make a list of where your documents live. Don't move them yet—just locate them. Junk drawer? Closet? Shoebox under your bed? This is step one. Because until you know where it all is, you can't begin to put it where it belongs.

___________________________________________

___________________________________________

___________________________________________

___________________________________________

___________________________________________

This is your first real grown-up mission if you choose to accept it — and no, it doesn't have to be perfect. Do your best. Start by checking off what you have on hand in one place, and don't stress about finishing it all in one sitting. This is just the beginning. You can circle back as you go, filling in the gaps and completing what's missing. The goal is progress, not perfection — and trust me, getting started is the hardest part. Look over the list below and check off the docs you can easily put your hands on (if you have one.)

Birth Certificate    Passport    Social Security card/number

Advanced Directive    Will/Trust    Car Insurance Policy

Life Insurance Policy    Living Will    Health Insurance

Business Insurance    Other Insurance

Gather them. Label them. Store them somewhere obvious: file folder, Google doc, binder of Shit You Need To Do Before You Die.

## Your Faves

This goes beyond your ICE (In Case of Emergency) contact and way past your "favorites" list on your phone. These are the people who would notice if you went dark — the ones who'd start texting, calling, or sending memes to make sure you're still breathing. Think beyond your inner circle: your favorite client who checks in every week, your cousin 2,000 miles away who you text every morning, your hairstylist who knows all your secrets, your best friend who can sense when something's off, even your son who's busy living his best life and doesn't always answer his phone. These are the humans who make up the rhythm of your real life — the ones who'd feel the silence if you suddenly disappeared.

List their names and contact information here so your family knows exactly who to reach out to if something happens. Because the only thing worse than bad news... is finding out about it on social media, or worse yet, in the obituary section. A few minutes of thought now can spare the people who love you from that shock — and make sure everyone who should know, does.

- Parents _______________________________________________

- Partner _______________________________________________

- Child _________________________________________________

- Other _________________________________________________

- Other _________________________________________________

- Other _________________________________________________

- Friend ________________________________________________

- Friend ________________________________________________

- Family ________________________________________________

- Family ________________________________________________

- Family ________________________________________________

- Family ________________________________________________

- Other _________________________________________________

- Other _________________________________________________

- Other _________________________________________________

- Other _________________________________________________

- Other _______________________________________________

## ❖ HR Contact Information _______________________________

_______________________________________________________

If you're employed, jot down your HR department's contact info, along with details about your benefits, payroll, retirement accounts, and any company perks that might be hiding in the fine print. You'd be amazed how much your HR rep knows about your life behind the scenes — sometimes more than your spouse does. They're the keepers of things like your 401(k), stock options, life insurance policies, and even unused PTO payouts that can make a real difference to your family later.

When something happens, HR is often the first domino that sets everything else in motion. They'll know who to contact, what paperwork to file, and what benefits your family might be entitled to — things no one else can easily untangle on their own.

I'll never forget the call I made the Monday after my husband died, before I'd even had my second cup of coffee. I didn't know what I was going to say — I just knew I had to call. And that one call unlocked everything: insurance information, beneficiary information, the documentation I'd need to file. It was the quiet reminder that while the world felt like it had stopped spinning, there was still a path forward — one small, practical step and one phone call at a time.

So yes, it might feel like a footnote now, but write it down. HR may not have the warmest bedside manner, but in moments like that, they're the people who help put the pieces back together.

# Section Summary – Get Personal

"Getting personal isn't about forms — it's about making sure your people get clarity, not chaos."

Use this space to jot down what you discovered in this chapter—the aha moments, the "oh crap" realizations, and the things you still need to handle. Write out your action items, follow-up calls, emails, and to-do's so you can actually complete what needs to get done here.

This chapter was all about getting organized — pulling together your personal data and documents so your future self (and your family) won't be left digging through drawers and guessing passwords. Write it down, track your progress, and keep that momentum rolling.

_______________________________________

_______________________________________

_______________________________________

_______________________________________

_______________________________________

_______________________________________

_______________________________________

_______________________________________

# CHAPTER 3

# DIGITAL ESTATE PLANNING

> *Don't ghost your loved ones online -leave the logins, not the chaos.*

*(Your Online Life After You Log Off for Good)*

Here's the brutal truth: most of us care more about our Wi-Fi password than our birth certificate. We'll spend 45 minutes resetting our Instagram login but couldn't tell you where our Social Security card is if our life depended on it. We bank online, shop online, stream online, date online, store every baby photo in "the cloud," and keep more secrets in our Notes app than we've ever told another human being.

And yet when it comes to planning for death? We act like our digital lives vanish into the ether the moment we do. News flash: they don't. They live on — every playlist, post, photo, and password — waiting for someone to make sense of the digital chaos you left behind.

Guess what? If you don't wrangle this now, your family will be stuck in digital purgatory. They'll be locked out of your accounts, frantically trying to guess your passwords ("Try her dog's name! No, her *first* dog!"), losing access to priceless memories, and arguing over whether it's "ethical" to reset your Netflix login. Meanwhile, your Facebook might turn into a weird ghost town where bots start tagging your friends in posts you didn't write.

Your digital life is real life now — it's your photo albums, your finances, your history, and in many ways, your legacy. So don't leave your family stranded at the login screen, fumbling through grief and Google forms. Give them a map — a clear, simple list that says, Here's where everything lives. *Here's how to find it. Here's how to close it when I'm gone.* It's not about control; it's about compassion. Because in today's world, logging out gracefully is just as important as logging in while you're still here.

## What Is a Digital Estate, Anyway?

Your digital estate = literally everything you log in to, pay for, or stash online. That means:

- Social media (Facebook, Instagram, TikTok, LinkedIn, X, etc.)

- Online banking + credit cards

- Investment + crypto accounts (Robinhood, Coinbase, your secret Bitcoin wallet)

- Reward programs + airline miles (yes, those can be inherited!)

- Subscriptions + memberships (Netflix, Prime, Peloton, even Costco)

- Cloud-stored files (Google Drive, iCloud, Dropbox, OneDrive)

- Email accounts (the keys to almost everything else)

- Photos, videos, music, ebooks, courses

- Domains + websites (that blog you started in 2008 still counts)

Even memberships and organizations — unions, alumni groups, professional associations, even Costco. Your amily will need to know which ones to cancel and which ones to keep. (But let's be real — no one's giving up the Costco card).

If you log in to it, it's part of your estate. Period.

## Why This Matters (a.k.a. The Digital Wake-Up Call)

The numbers don't lie:

- 70% of Americans have no plan for their digital assets (AARP, 2023).

- Airlines estimate trillions of frequent flier miles are lost every year because families didn't know they could claim them.

- A McAfee study found the average American's digital assets are worth $55,000. For that amount you could put a new car in your garage.

- And Google alone has 2.5 billion Gmail accounts— many of which become ghost towns the moment someone dies.

Translation: your digital junk drawer is basically a vault of money and memories. And unless you leave the keys, it stays locked.

## The Nightmare Scenario

Picture this: you die, and no one can access your bank logins. Bills don't get paid, mortgages default, your Spotify subscription keeps auto-billing your debit card... oh, and those 4,000 family photos? Gone forever when your iCloud subscription lapses.

Or worse: your Facebook turns into a zombie account where spammy bots start DM-ing your friends about cryptocurrency. That's not a "digital legacy." That's a digital horror story.

## Digital Estate Prep 101 (a.k.a. Don't Be a Ghost Online)

**Step 1: Take Inventory**
List every single account—banking, email, cloud, social, crypto, subscriptions. (Hint: scroll through your phone and browser autofill—you'll be shocked how many accounts you've forgotten exist.)

## Step 2: Organize Logins

Put usernames + passwords in a password manager (1Password, LastPass, Bitwarden). *Do not leave them "in your head."* You are not immortal.

_______________________________________________

_______________________________________________

_______________________________________________

_______________________________________________

_______________________________________________

_______________________________________________

_______________________________________________

_______________________________________________

_______________________________________________

_______________________________________________

## Step 3: Appoint a Digital Executor

Pick someone smart enough not to click on "Hot Singles Near You." They'll handle closing accounts, moving files, cancelling subscriptions, and saving the important stuff.

Name and contact including phone, email, and address.

_______________________________________________

_______________________________________________

_______________________________________________

_______________________________________________

**Step 4: Set Social Media Instructions**
Most platforms let you do one of three options.

*Memorialize your profile (like a digital gravestone):*

When you're gone, your social media doesn't just vanish — it lingers, frozen in time. Memorializing your profile turns it into a kind of digital gravestone: a place where friends and family can share memories, post photos, and celebrate your life without worrying about hackers or birthday reminders popping up years later. It locks your account, protects your content, and lets your online story stay intact — a final, virtual gathering place for the people who miss you most.

*Delete your account (clean slate)*

Not everyone wants to leave a digital shrine behind — and that's okay. Choosing to delete your accounts after you die is the online version of turning off the lights and locking the door. It wipes your data, your photos, your posts — everything. No digital ghosts, no awkward "Happy Birthday in Heaven" messages, no half-frozen timeline gathering dust. It's a clean exit, a conscious choice to let your story live on in memory, not metadata.

*Appoint a legacy contact (Facebook, Google, Apple all offer this)*

Think of a legacy contact as your digital executor — the person who steps in to manage your online life when you no longer can. Platforms like Facebook, Google, and Apple let you officially name someone to handle things like memorializing your page, saving photos, or closing accounts. It's the modern version of leaving someone your house keys, only this time it's for your digital world. Choose someone you trust — someone who'll treat your online presence with the same care they'd give your real one.

## Step 5: Handle Financial + Rewards

Document bank logins, crypto wallets, investment accounts, airline miles, hotel points. Yes, reward points can be transferred—don't leave free vacations on the table.

| Company | Account # | Login |
| --- | --- | --- |
|  |  |  |
|  |  |  |
|  |  |  |
|  |  |  |
|  |  |  |
|  |  |  |
|  |  |  |
|  |  |  |
|  |  |  |
|  |  |  |
|  |  |  |
|  |  |  |
|  |  |  |
|  |  |  |
|  |  |  |
|  |  |  |
|  |  |  |

## Step 6: Don't Forget the Small Stuff

Document bank logins, crypto wallets, investment accounts, airline miles, hotel points. Yes, reward points can be transferred—don't leave free vacations on the table.

| Company | Account # | Login |
|---|---|---|
|  |  |  |
|  |  |  |
|  |  |  |
|  |  |  |
|  |  |  |
|  |  |  |
|  |  |  |
|  |  |  |
|  |  |  |
|  |  |  |
|  |  |  |
|  |  |  |
|  |  |  |
|  |  |  |
|  |  |  |
|  |  |  |

# Quick Story: The Lost Photos Disaster

I knew a family who lost every childhood picture because Dad kept them all in his personal iCloud account. No one knew the login. When the subscription lapsed, so did the memories. Thousands of photos—Christmas mornings, graduations, baby's first steps—gone in a digital blink.

That's not just careless. That's cruel. Don't be that person.

## Section Summary – Digital Estate Planning

"Don't become a ghost online. Leave the keys so your family doesn't get locked out of your digital life."

Write down your top 5 digital accounts (banking, email, cloud, social, subscriptions).

If you disappeared tomorrow, could your family access them?

Yes or no.

Then pick your digital executor. (Hint: if they still use "password123," it's not them.)

1.______________________________________________

2.______________________________________________

3.______________________________________________

4. _______________________________________________________

5. _______________________________________________________

Digital Executor: _________________________________________

## Digital Estate Worksheet

**The "Where the Hell Is the Password?" Master List**
This is your one-stop cheat sheet for the digital side of your life — your online treasure map, your key to the kingdom, your "oh thank God they wrote this down" document. Everything from your bank logins to your Google Photos account lives here. Fill it out, keep it somewhere safe, and for the love of all things encrypted, tell your digital executor where it is.

Pro tip: do not leave this sitting on your desk in plain sight unless you want your teenage nephew "accidentally" upgrading his Xbox subscription on your dime or your sister Venmoing herself "reimbursement" money for something you definitely didn't authorize.

If you're even a little tech-savvy, consider creating a password-protected Google Sheet or using a password manager like 1Password or Bitwarden. You can share limited access with your digital executor — the one person you trust not to panic and post "She's dead but still streaming Spotify Premium" to your account.

And remember: this list isn't just about logins. It's about access — to your life, your photos, your memories, your subscriptions, even your social media goodbye posts (because yes, one day someone will have to decide whether your final Facebook update says "Life Event: I Died" or not).

This simple little list might not seem important now, but when the time comes, it will save your family from hours

of guessing, tears, and frantic tech support calls that start with, "So... my mom's dead, but we really need her iCloud password."

### Section 1: Social Media & Communication

## Facebook

User name/email_____________________________________

Password/hint_______________________________________

Delete/memorialize/appoint legacy?_____________________

## Meta Business Suite

User name/email_____________________________________

Password/hint_______________________________________

Delete/memorialize/appoint legacy?_____________________

## Instagram

User name/email_____________________________________

Password/hint_______________________________________

Delete/memorialize/appoint legacy?_____________________

## X/Twitter

User name/email_____________________________________

Password/hint_______________________________________

Delete/memorialize/appoint legacy?_____________________

## TikTok

User name/email_______________________________________

Password/hint_________________________________________

Delete/memorialize/appoint legacy?_____________________

## LinkedIn

User name/email_______________________________________

Password/hint_________________________________________

Delete/memorialize/appoint legacy?_____________________

## Email accounts: Gmail, Yahoo, Outlook, etc.

Delete/memorialize/appoint legacy?_____________________

#1 User name/email____________________________________

Password/hint_________________________________________

Delete/memorialize/appoint legacy?_____________________

#2 User name/email____________________________________

Password/hint_________________________________________

Delete/memorialize/appoint legacy?_____________________

#3 User name/email____________________________________

Password/hint_________________________________________

Delete/memorialize/appoint legacy?_____________________

#4 User name/email_______________________________________________

Password/hint__________________________________________________

Delete/memorialize/appoint legacy?_____________________________

**Other Social Accounts**

### Pinterest

User name/email_______________________________________________

Password/hint__________________________________________________

Delete/memorialize/appoint legacy?_____________________________

### Reddit

User name/email_______________________________________________

Password/hint__________________________________________________

Delete/memorialize/appoint legacy?_____________________________

### Rumble

User name/email_______________________________________________

Password/hint__________________________________________________

Delete/memorialize/appoint legacy?_____________________________

### Other

User name/email_______________________________________________

Password/hint__________________________________________________

Delete/memorialize/appoint legacy?_____________________________

### Other

User name/email_______________________________________________

Password/hint_______________________________________________

Delete/memorialize/appoint legacy?_______________________________

**Other**

User name/email_____________________________________________

Password/hint_______________________________________________

Delete/memorialize/appoint legacy?_______________________________

*Password Hint = something only your executor would understand. (Example: "My dog's weird nickname + birth year.")

### Section 2: Financial Accounts

Types of accounts listed as financial.

*Banking, Investment, Venmo, CashApp, Coinbase, Binance, etc.*

### #1 (Example) Institution/Platform: Bank of America

| | |
|---|---|
| Account type | (Banking/Crypto/Investment/Other) |
| User Name/ID | MamaN66 |
| Password/Hint | High School mascot followed by mom's birthdate |
| Executor Instructions: | Close/Transfer/Maintain   CLOSE |
| Notes | None |

**#2 Institution/Platform**_______________________________________

Account type_______________________________________________

User Name/ID_______________________________________________

Password/Hint______________________________________________

Executor Instructions:______________________________________

Notes______________________________________________________

**#3 Institution/Platform**_______________________________________

Account type_______________________________________________

User Name/ID_______________________________________________

Password/Hint______________________________________________

Executor Instructions:______________________________________

Notes______________________________________________________

**#4 Institution/Platform**_______________________________________

Account type_______________________________________________

User Name/ID_______________________________________________

Password/Hint______________________________________________

Executor Instructions:______________________________________

Notes______________________________________________________

**#5 Institution/Platform**_______________________________________

Account type_______________________________________________

User Name/ID_______________________________________________

Password/Hint______________________________________________

Executor Instructions:______________________________________

Notes______________________________________________________

**#6 Institution/Platform**___________________________

Account type______________________________________

User Name/ID______________________________________

Password/Hint______________________________________

Executor Instructions:______________________________

Notes______________________________________________

**#7 Institution/Platform**___________________________

Account type______________________________________

User Name/ID______________________________________

Password/Hint______________________________________

Executor Instructions:______________________________

Notes______________________________________________

**#8 Institution/Platform**___________________________

Account type______________________________________

User Name/ID______________________________________

Password/Hint______________________________________

Executor Instructions:______________________________

Notes______________________________________________

## Section 3: Subscriptions & Memberships

This is where you list all the services that quietly bill you every month — Netflix, Amazon Prime, Apple Music, Spotify, Pandora, gym memberships, Peloton, upgrades — all the things that keep your digital life running. Many of these connect through your digital wallet (Google Play, Apple ID, or iTunes), so include those login details too.

This is also a great place to list your cell phone carrier, account number, and password. Because let's be honest—nobody wants your phone ringing nonstop with spammers trying to sell you an extended warranty or a "free windshield replacement" after you're gone. One simple list here saves your loved ones from that headache (and your ghost from endless robocalls).

## Service

**#1 Account type/App Name**_______________________________

User name/Email_______________________________

Password_______________________________

Cancel/Transfer?_______________________________

Notes_______________________________

**#2 Account type/App Name**_______________________________

User name/Email_______________________________

Password_______________________________

Cancel/Transfer?_______________________________

Notes_______________________________

**#3 Account type/App Name**_______________________________

User name/Email_______________________________

Password_______________________________

Cancel/Transfer?_______________________________

Notes_______________________________

**#4 Account type/App Name**_______________________________

User name/Email_______________________________

Password______________________________________________________

Cancel/Transfer?________________________________________________

Notes__________________________________________________________

## #5 Account type/App Name_____________________________________

User name/Email_________________________________________________

Password______________________________________________________

Cancel/Transfer?________________________________________________

Notes__________________________________________________________

## #6 Account type/App Name_____________________________________

User name/Email_________________________________________________

Password______________________________________________________

Cancel/Transfer?________________________________________________

Notes__________________________________________________________

## #7 Account type/App Name_____________________________________

User name/Email_________________________________________________

Password______________________________________________________

Cancel/Transfer?________________________________________________

Notes__________________________________________________________

## #8 Account type/App Name_____________________________________

User name/Email_________________________________________________

Password______________________________________________________

Cancel/Transfer?________________________________________________

Notes__________________________________________________________

**#9 Account type/App Name**_______________________________

User name/Email_______________________________________

Password_____________________________________________

Cancel/Transfer?______________________________________

Notes________________________________________________

**#10 Account type/App Name**______________________________

User name/Email_______________________________________

Password_____________________________________________

Cancel/Transfer?______________________________________

Notes________________________________________________

### Section 4: Cloud Storage & Digital Files

Google drive, iCloud, Drop Box One Drive, Music files, etc.

**#1 Platform**___________________________________________

User name/Email_______________________________________

Password_____________________________________________

Cancel/Transfer?______________________________________

Notes________________________________________________

**#2 Platform**___________________________________________

User name/Email_______________________________________

Password_____________________________________________

Cancel/Transfer?______________________________________

Notes________________________________________________

**#4 Platform**_______________________________________

User name/Email_______________________________________

Password_______________________________________

Cancel/Transfer?_______________________________________

Notes_______________________________________

**#5 Platform**_______________________________________

User name/Email_______________________________________

Password_______________________________________

Cancel/Transfer?_______________________________________

Notes_______________________________________

**#6 Platform**_______________________________________

User name/Email_______________________________________

Password_______________________________________

Cancel/Transfer?_______________________________________

Notes_______________________________________

**#7 Platform**_______________________________________

User name/Email_______________________________________

Password_______________________________________

Cancel/Transfer?_______________________________________

Notes_______________________________________

**#8 Platform**_______________________________________

User name/Email_______________________________________

Password_______________________________________

**Section 5: Domains, Websites, & Online Businesses**

Examples – Websites, Etsy Shops, Shopify Stores, Printify, etc.

**#1 Domain/Site**_______________________________

User name/Email_________________________________

Password______________________________________

Notes on Renewal/Transfer_______________________

Notes _________________________________________

**Section 6: Reward Points & Travel**

This includes everything from hotels, airlines, rental cars, rewards membership plans, etc.

**#1 Program**_________________________________

User name/Email_________________________________

Password______________________________________

Cancel/Transfer?________________________________

Notes_________________________________________

**#2 Platform**_________________________________

User name/Email_________________________________

Password______________________________________

Cancel/Transfer?________________________________

Notes_________________________________________

### #3 Platform______________________________________________

User name/Email______________________________________

Password______________________________________________

Cancel/Transfer?______________________________________

Notes__________________________________________________

### #4 Platform______________________________________________

User name/Email______________________________________

Password______________________________________________

Cancel/Transfer?______________________________________

Notes__________________________________________________

### #5 Platform______________________________________________

User name/Email______________________________________

Password______________________________________________

Cancel/Transfer?______________________________________

Notes__________________________________________________

### #6 Platform______________________________________________

User name/Email______________________________________

Password______________________________________________

Cancel/Transfer?______________________________________

Notes__________________________________________________

**#7 Platform**________________________________________

User name/Email_______________________________________

Password____________________________________________

Cancel/Transfer?______________________________________

Notes_______________________________________________

**#8 Platform**________________________________________

User name/Email_______________________________________

Password____________________________________________

Cancel/Transfer?______________________________________

Notes_______________________________________________

**The Final Step: Choose Your Digital Executor**

Examples – Websites, Etsy Shops, Shopify Stores, Printify, etc.

Name:_______________________________________________

Relationship:_________________________________________

Contact Info:_________________________________________

**Reminder:** Don't pick the cousin who still clicks on "Congratulations, you've won an iPad!"

Fill in at least one account from each section of your digital life today. Seriously — start now, not "someday." Later has a way of never showing up, and your future self (and your family) will thank you when they can actually access what they need without calling tech support or hiring a hacker. Start with the basics: your email, your main bank login, your favorite streaming service, and your phone account. Then keep adding over time. Every detail you record — a password, a hint, a recovery email — is one less locked door for the people who'll be handling things when you can't. Think of it as leaving a breadcrumb trail through your digital world, so no one has to wander lost in a maze of logins and "forgot password" links.

### ★ Real Life Stories: Digital Disasters

**The Lost Photos**
After John passed away, his family discovered thousands of family photos locked in his iCloud account. No one knew the password. The subscription lapsed, the files deleted. Years of memories — gone.

**The Crypto Vanish**
Ron invested in crypto but never documented his wallet keys. After his sudden death, his family had no way to access it. Over $1,000,000 disappeared into the blockchain abyss.

**The Smooth Transfer**
Maria left her daughter a list of all her logins and named her as digital executor. Within a week, her accounts were closed, her photos were backed up, and her online business transitioned smoothly. Zero chaos.

**Lesson:** Treat your digital life like your real life. If it matters to you, protect it.

Use this space to capture what you learned in this chapter and what still needs to get done. Jot down your discoveries, reminders, passwords to update, and any "oh crap, I forgot about that account" moments. Write out your follow-up tasks, emails, and calls so nothing slips through the cracks.

This chapter was about **getting your digital life in order** — organizing logins, passwords, and online accounts so your loved ones don't get locked out of your memories, money, or music playlists. Treat it like a digital treasure map and finish the list while it's all still fresh.

# CHAPTER 4

# LIFE INSURANCE: LOVE LETTER OR WASTE OF MONEY?

Let's get real: most of us will shell out $12.99/month to keep Netflix rolling, $19.99 for "extended warranty protection" on an air fryer, and tack on cell phone insurance without blinking. But when it comes to life insurance? Suddenly it's "too expensive" or "probably a scam." Priorities, people.

Here's the cold hard facts: if anyone depends on your paycheck—kids, spouse, partner, aging parents, even the dog—then yes, you need life insurance or an equivalent financial plan. Especially if you're the high income earner in the family. Because when you're gone, so is your income. And without a plan? Your family's left scrambling.

I learned this the hardest way possible. My husband died suddenly at 54—of all places, at Disneyland. Our monthly expenses were close to $12,000 at the time—five kids, a big mortgage, two dogs, a grocery bill nearing the national debt,

several cars, a motor yacht on the coast, and college and weddings on the horizon. If it weren't for his life insurance policy, we would've lost everything. Life insurance wasn't a "nice-to-have." It was the only reason we didn't drown.

Life insurance isn't about you. It's about the people left picking up the pieces after you're gone.

## The Different Flavors of Life Insurance

Both *Life Happens and the Consumer Financial Protection Bureau* remind us that life insurance isn't one-size-fits-all. Think of it like ordering at Starbucks—lots of options, wildly different price tags. Here's a breakdown:

**1. Term Life (the "no-BS" option)**

- Covers you for a set time (10, 20, 30 years).

- **Best for:** covering your "big expense" years—mortgage, kids, college.

- **Pros:** Simple, affordable, big coverage for small bucks.

- **Cons:** Temporary. Outlive it, and congrats—you get nothing.

**2. Whole Life (the "forever" plan)**

- Lasts your whole life (as long as you pay). Builds "cash value" you can borrow.

- **Pros:** Never expires, predictable, has a savings component.

- **Cons:** Expensive AF. Like, 10x more than term.

### 3. Universal Life (flexible but fussy)

- Adjustable premiums, builds cash value.

- **Pros:** Flexibility + growth potential.

- **Cons:** Fees and complexity. If you underfund it, it can collapse.

### 4. Variable Life (insurance meets Wall Street)

- Includes investment accounts. Your value grows—or tanks—with the market.

- **Pros:** Growth potential, tax perks.

- **Cons:** High risk + high fees. Not for people who panic when the market dips.

### 5. Final Expense (a.k.a. burial insurance)

- Small policy ($5k–$25k) just to cover funeral costs.

- **Pros:** Easy approval, guaranteed payout.

- **Cons:** Pricey for what you get.

## How Much Coverage Do You Actually Need?

**Rule of thumb**

About **10x your annual income** – examples:
- Make $70k/year? Aim for ~$700k.
- Make $100k/year? About a million.

**Scenario 1:** You make $80k. If you die, that income disappears. A $1 million policy, wisely invested, could provide ~$40k/year in returns + Social Security benefits—covering most expenses for decades for your family.

> **Scenario 2:** You make $50k, spouse stays home. Even $500k could cover the mortgage and give your partner breathing room.

**Scenario 3:** You're single, no kids. Do you need $1 million? Nope. But at least leave enough for final expenses so your friends and family aren't setting up a Go-Fund-Me or Venmo-ing each other to cover your funeral.

## Beneficiaries: The Soap Opera

Here's where it gets sticky. Once upon a time, naming your spouse and kids as beneficiaries was simple — tidy even. You had a family, you left them your stuff, the end. But now? Welcome to the modern family circus. Blended families, ex-spouses, stepkids, pets with Instagram followings, and yes—even that charity you drunkenly promised half your estate to at a gala three years ago—are all in the mix.

And that's before you factor in human emotions. The "I thought I was your favorite" crowd? They'll be watching like it's the season finale of Succession. If you're not crystal clear, you're basically handing out front-row tickets to a family feud.

Maybe you adore your stepdaughter yet your biological son still hasn't forgiven you for missing his middle school talent show. Maybe your second spouse is wonderful but your kids secretly call her "gold digger" behind her back. Or maybe you've got that one sibling who's been "borrowing" money since the Clinton administration. Whatever your situation, don't let assumptions write your story.

This is your chance to be deliberate. *Who actually depends on you?* Who do you want to bless when you're gone? And who—let's be honest—would you rather leave with fond memories than a check?

A will or policy is more than just paperwork. It's your final mic drop — your last chance to make sure the right people (and causes) benefit from the life you built. So take your time. Think it through. And maybe, just maybe, resist the urge to name your cat as your sole heir (unless she's really earned it).

## My Real Life Story: The Surprise Beneficiary

We'd been married for more than 18 years when my husband died. He had worked for the same company the entire time we were married (and several years before that). Every year, without fail, he filled out his benefits paperwork—writing my name as his beneficiary in the same all-caps handwriting he had since 2nd grade. If he was anything, he was detailed and thorough. Now I see it for what it was—his own way of making sure I would be okay.

Just days after he passed, I called his HR representative. rep. She was kind, and said someone from benefits would reach out. Days went by. Nothing. I called again. Still nothing. Finally, I got a call from a woman named Karen—the kind of voice that says she's about to deliver bad news wrapped in policies. She said she couldn't share any information with me. I wasn't his beneficiary.

I went numb. Everything was muffled. I could hear myself screaming but it felt like it was coming from someone else. Then I lost it. "What do you mean? We were married! I saw him fill out those forms for 18 years. I've seen the statements every year. I'm his wife."

This was just the beginning of the mountain of red tape. There was a hidden clause buried deep in his divorce decree called a QDRO—a Qualified Domestic Relations Order. It stated that, in the event of his death, his ex-wife would be treated as his spouse. (Instead of me.) And in the world of legal fine print, if this were a card game, a QDRO would be the wildcard that trumped every HR form he'd ever signed.

I was crushed. Still in shock that he was never walking through the door again and now a stranger from his company was telling me I wasn't recognized as his spouse. Somehow, I needed to find the focus and strength to go into battle—to fight for what he had secured for me. Grief didn't wait for me to get organized. I was shattered, exhausted, and now forced to become a warrior in a fight I never saw coming. It was a harsh, expensive heartbreaking lesson in how love may last a lifetime, but paperwork can outlive us all.

Bottom line: beneficiaries = those who are in your life that you actually want to take care of. And remember—you can change them anytime.

Review them regularly. Beneficiaries. Old divorce papers. Fine print. Life changes fast.

# Excuses People Use to Avoid Life Insurance (And Why They're Lame)

**"It's too expensive."**
Nope. Most term policies cost less than your monthly latte habit. If you can afford Hulu, you can afford coverage.

**"I'm healthy. I don't need it yet."**
Exactly why it's cheap right now. Wait until you're older and your premiums will eat you alive.

**"I'll just save money instead."**
Cute. But let's be real—if saving was that easy, your "rainy day fund" wouldn't look like $84 and some loose change you found under the sofa cushion. Insurance bridges the gap while you build wealth.

**"I don't have dependents."**
Great, but funerals still cost money. Someone's got to cover the box, the flowers, or your cryogenic freezing to turn you into a popsicle. Don't make your friends pass the collection plate.

**"It's a scam."**
The only scam is pretending your family won't need help if you're gone. You die → your family gets financial security. Simple contract, not a conspiracy.

Not everyone can (or wants to) buy a policy. So here are other ways to make sure your family is protected:

- Dedicated Savings Account: A cash cushion earmarked for "just in case."

- Investments: IRAs, 401(k)s, brokerage accounts— assets that pass to your heirs.

- Property: Homes, rentals, or real estate that can be sold or leveraged.

- Employer Benefits: Some companies include basic life insurance (1–2x your salary).

- Trusts: A living trust ensures assets go where you want them.

## Section Summary – Life Insurance

> *Insurance isn't about you - it's the love letter that keeps your people afloat when you're gone.*

## Mini Homework Prompt:

Write down your annual income × 10 = your ballpark coverage.

- List your dependents. (This doesn't just include children under 18.) It's who would be financially screwed if you were gone.

_______________________________________________

_______________________________________________

_______________________________________________

_______________________________________________

_______________________________________________

- Write down your current coverage (if any) and when you last updated it.

- If you don't have coverage, jot one alternative (savings, investments, property) you could set up in the next 6 months.

_______________________________________________

_______________________________________________

_______________________________________________

## Real Life Story: The Family That Lost Everything

David had an insurance policy but missed his one premium payment. He was young and healthy, and the last thing he thought about was death. He had finally climbed the ladder of success. He was in the middle of building a mansion just outside of town. Then—out of nowhere—he had a massive heart attack. He was gone in an instant at 42. No warning, no time to say good-bye and no insurance.

He was so busy running his business, dealing with contractors and keeping his head above water that he forgot to make his premium payment. Within months, his wife had to sell the incomplete house to an investor. She picked up two jobs just to pay rent on the small apartment she found. The kids had to leave their private schools. Vacations? College funds? All gone. Their entire lifestyle evaporated overnight, and the only thing she kept saying was, *"If only he hadn't missed that payment, things would be different."*

Remember: life insurance isn't about preparing for "if" you die. It's about protecting the people you love for when you do. One family lost everything because they skipped it. Don't let that be yours.

## Real Life Story: The Family That Stayed Afloat

On the flip side, another family I know faced a similar tragedy. The dad passed away suddenly at 49. It was devastating. But here's the difference: he had a $750,000 life insurance policy. That payout meant his wife didn't have to sell their home. The kids stayed in their same schools. College savings stayed intact. She was able to heal and even had enough breathing room to grieve instead of immediately scramble to find a second job.

It didn't take away the heartbreak, but it prevented financial disaster from adding to her grief. That's what life insurance really is: not a jackpot, not a scam—just a lifeline.

Use this section to jot down what you uncovered in this chapter—names, numbers, and next steps. Record your to-do's, calls to make, quotes to compare, and any policies

This chapter was about life insurance—your ultimate love letter. Make note of who's covered, who's not, and what gaps you need to fill. Write down questions for your agent, update your beneficiaries, and make sure your family will be protected when it matters most.

# CHAPTER 5

# HERE'S TO YOUR HEALTH

> *Cheers to the messy miracle of being alive-and the wisdom to plan for when we're not.*

*(a.k.a. Who Gets the Final Say and Access "To The Plug")*

Let's be honest: "advance directive" sounds like something your doctor whispers out of the corner of his mouth while scanning the waiting room to see if anyone heard him. And no, it's not the directive that comes after you reach level one, and it's not a new app. Most important—it's not optional if you want to save your family from turning into a Lifetime drama.

An advance directive is simply your way of saying—in writing—what you want (and don't want for your health) when you can't speak for yourself. It's not glamorous, but neither is your cousin crying in the ICU waiting room while your mom and spouse battle over whether to pull the plug.

Most people avoid this step because it feels heavy. Too serious. Too soon. They shove the idea into the same dusty mental drawer as their almost-expired passport and those college jeans they swear they'll fit back into. But here's the thing, if you don't write this down, someone else will decide for you. And trust me, the loudest voice in the room doesn't always make the best decision in your best interest. This is where most people close this book. Because talking about their hypothetical far off in the-distant demise is one thing. But talking about Junior pulling the plug is another.  So if you don't have the guts to write it down, here's your chance to close this book and pass it on to a friend who is more courageous than you are.

## The Building Blocks of an Advance Directive

Before we dive into the forms and fine print, here's the big picture: this is where you call the shots. Your **advance directive** is essentially your healthcare game plan — the roadmap for what you want (and don't want) if you can't speak for yourself. It's not morbid, it's mature — and it saves the people you love from having to make impossible choices in a crisis. Think of it as your own personal "Choose Your Own Adventure" for medical care... only this time, you don't get to flip back if you don't like the ending. These are the main players:

**01  Living Will (Your medical wish list)**

- Says exactly what treatments you want—or want to avoid—if you're seriously ill, unconscious, or at the end of life.

- Machines forever? Pain meds even if they shorten life? Feeding tubes? You decide now, so no one else has to play psychic later.

- Kicks in only when you can't speak for yourself.

**02  Healthcare Proxy / Medical Power of Attorney (Your MVP)**

- The person you appoint to make decisions when you can't.

- Why it matters: paperwork can't cover every "what if." Your proxy fills in the blanks.

- Pick someone level-headed and strong. Not your cousin who cries at commercials or the friend who still falls for the scammer text about the toll road fees he owes.

### 03  Do Not Resuscitate Order (DNR)

- A doctor's order that says: no CPR, no heroics if your heart stops.

- Some people want every possible intervention. Others would rather exit quietly without cracked ribs and tubes everywhere. Your choice, your call. Note: Read the fine print. There are different versions of DNR including AND, DNI, DRN-CC. But this alphabet soup means nothing if you don't look into it and get it together.

### 04  POLST / MOLST (Physician Orders for Life-Sustaining Treatment)

- A signed medical order for people facing serious illness.

- Tells emergency responders exactly what to do—or not do.

- Think of it as a "frontline" version of your living will.

### 05  Organ Donation: The Ultimate Parting Gift

You can't take your organs with you, and if you don't make your wishes clear now, your family may have to make that call in the middle of a crisis. That's not fair to them.

How to make it official: choose it on your driver's license, register online at OrganDonor.gov, and — most importantly — write it into your advance directive and tell your family. When they know it's your decision, they can honor it without hesitation.

Your story may end, but pieces of you can help someone else's life continue. It's a personal choice and decision. And for those who choose it, it's a legacy worth writing down.

## What Happens If You Don't Have One?

**Accident leaves you unconscious.** Spouse says keep you alive, parents say let you go. Cue drama, lawyers, and resentment that lasts decades.

**Illness takes your voice.** Kids disagree about treatment. They stop speaking to each other. Holidays ruined forever.

**Decline without a DNR.** You're resuscitated over and over, hooked up to machines you never wanted, and your last days look nothing like you'd hoped.

No directive = chaos. A directive = clarity.

## How to Create One
## (Easier Than Ordering DoorDash)

**Lawyer up.** They'll draft, file, and make it airtight.

**DIY.** Every state has free forms. Fill them out, sign, and get them notarized or witnessed.

**Once you've got it:**

- Keep the original somewhere obvious, ideally with the other documents in this kit (not buried in the junk drawer under batteries and expired coupons).

- Give copies to your proxy, your doctor, and anyone who matters.

- Carry a wallet card so emergency staff know it exists.

## Review & Refresh

Life shifts, people come and go, health changes. Review once a year. Set a calendar reminder. Update it if your health changes, your proxy drops the ball, or your relationships take a turn (divorces and new partners make for awkward paperwork if you don't).

## Real-Life Stories

- **The Family at Peace**
  Maria's dad had everything in writing. When a stroke left him unable to communicate, his wishes were clear: no feeding tubes, comfort care only. His family could just be with him—no guilt, no fighting, just time together.

- **The Family at War**
  Jim never wrote one. After a car accident left him in a coma, his wife wanted life support, his kids wanted it ended. The battle got so ugly it went to court. Jim lingered for months, and the family still isn't speaking years later.

- **The Hidden Blessing**
  Alyssa, just 39, had cancer that spread quickly. Because she set up a proxy and DNR, her best friend could follow her wishes. It was brutal, but her family called it the greatest gift: clarity and peace during the most difficult time.

# Section Summary – Here's to Your Health

"An advance directive is basically you saying, 'You're welcome'—before anyone starts arguing in the waiting room."

## Mini Homework Prompt:

- Write down one treatment you'd want and one you'd refuse if you couldn't speak.

______________________________________________

______________________________________________

______________________________________________

- Write the name of one person you'd trust to make decisions.

______________________________________________

______________________________________________

- Put a yearly reminder in your phone to review it.

Use this space to capture what stood out in this chapter—decisions, details, and anything you still need to clarify. Write down follow-up calls, appointments, and conversations you need to have with your doctor, proxy, or family.

This chapter was about **your health and your voice when you can't speak for yourself.** Note where your advance directive is stored, who your healthcare proxy is, and any updates you want to make to your wishes. This is your roadmap for peace of mind—write it, share it, and keep it.

# CHAPTER 6

# APPOINTING YOUR M.V.P.

> *When I die, I want to be thrown out of an airplane wearing a Superman costume.*

*(a.k.a. Your Power of Attorney)*

Okay, maybe you won't be skydiving in tights anytime soon, but let's talk about your real-life superhero: your Power of Attorney. Not the kind who sues people or chases ambulances. The kind who swoops in when you can't — pays the bills, talks to doctors, keep the lights on, and generally prevents your life from collapsing like a bad Jenga tower.

You might think: *Power of Attorney sounds terrifying*, like something ripped straight from a courtroom drama. But in reality? It's just a document that says, *"If I can't handle this, here's who's in charge."* Think of it as naming your personal M.V.P. — the one who gets the ball when you're benched.

Without it? Welcome to absolute chaos. Picture this: you're in a hospital bed, unable to speak. Your spouse and kids are in the hallway arguing about who should handle the bills. Your sister wants to "wait and see," your brother thinks he's the boss because he's loud, and your best friend is standing there with common sense but no legal authority to do a thing. Meanwhile, the mortgage company doesn't care, the utilities keep running, and your dog still needs food.

So your family turns to the courts — the land of red tape, legal fees, and endless waiting. It's a place colder than the meat section at Costco and about as fast as dial-up internet. In other words, a *nightmare.* And all of it could've been avoided with one simple piece of paper.

Your Power of Attorney is your pinch hitter, your backup quarterback, your "in case of emergency, break glass" human. They can handle everything from signing your name on financial documents to making healthcare decisions when you can't. It's not morbid — it's smart. Because life has a way of throwing curveballs, and this ensures that when it does, someone you trust is ready to catch them.

So pick your person wisely. This isn't about who's closest or who'll be the most emotional — it's about who can keep their cool when things get messy. Someone responsible, level-headed, and maybe a little bossy (in a good way). Your M.V.P. should be the person who'll step up, not back down. Because when life gets complicated, you want a hero who knows exactly what to do — and has the paperwork to prove it.

## POA Is Pure Gold

A POA isn't just about death—it's about life's messy in-betweens. The stuff no one plans for but happens anyway:

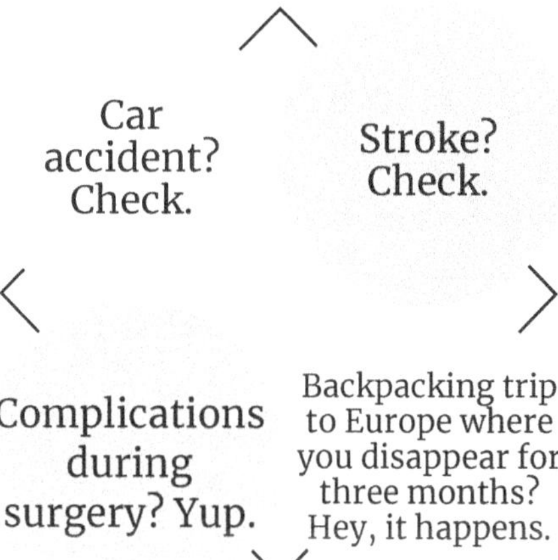

While you're out of commission, your POA keeps things moving:

**Bills paid.** (Because your mortgage company won't accept "coma" as a payment method.)

**Health decisions made.** (By someone you trust, not by Aunt Linda who thinks essential oils cure everything.)

**Your voice respected.** (Because you literally picked the person to speak for you.)

## The Different Types of POA (a.k.a. Pick Your Flavor)

**General POA**

- Covers broad financial/legal stuff.

- Great if you're traveling or deployed.

- Dies the second you're incapacitated. (Which is, ironically, when you'd need a POA most.)

**Durable POA**

- This is the heavy lifter. Keeps going even if you can't.

- Pays bills, files taxes, makes healthcare calls.

- If you only do one type, do this one.

### Medical POA / Healthcare Proxy

- Handles your healthcare choices specifically.

- Works best when paired with a living will.

- Example: deciding "yes" to pain relief but "hell no" to 12 machines keeping you alive indefinitely.

### Limited / Special POA

- For one specific thing.

- Example: You're selling your house while abroad and need someone to sign closing papers.

### Springing POA

- Only kicks in under specific conditions, like when two doctors sign off that you're incapacitated.

- Pro: you stay fully in charge until you can't.

- Con: delays. And do you really want your family waiting on paperwork while your power bill goes unpaid?

## Choosing Your MVP

This isn't a casual pick, like naming someone your emergency contact for your AppleID. You're handing over the keys to your life. Pick someone who is:

**Trustworthy. (Translation:** not the cousin who "borrowed" your credit card.)

**Strong.** They may have to stare down emotional relatives and say, "No, this is what he or she wanted."

**Available.** Local helps. Emergencies don't wait for long-distance calls or time zones.

**Willing.** Don't just slap their name down. Ask them. Make sure they're up for it.

And for the love of sanity, name a backup. Your star player could get sick, move, or just flake out. Always have someone on the bench.

## What Happens If You Don't Bother?

- Bills pile up. Accounts freeze. Foreclosure letters roll in.

- Courts step in. Judges decide who's in charge, not you.

- Family drama explodes. Siblings brawl, in-laws interfere, and your medical care gets stuck in limbo.

*Translation:* no POA = the perfect storm for legal red tape and family feuds.

## Getting It Done (a.k.a. Pro Planning Tip)

△ Choose your MVP (and your backup).

1. _______________________________________________

2. _______________________________________________

△ Decide what powers they'll have (money, health, or both).

1. _______________________________________________

2. _______________________________________________

3. _______________________________________________

△ Use a lawyer or grab your state's free forms online.

△ Sign them in front of witnesses or a notary.

△ Give copies to your MVP, doctor, and family. Keep one with your important docs.

△ Done. Cross it off the list.

## POA in Real Life: Why It Matters

**The Smooth Operator**
Renee had a durable POA. When she had a stroke, her daughter seamlessly paid bills, managed insurance, and kept everything afloat. No shut-off notices. No legal wrangling. Just smooth sailing.

**The Financial Freeze**
Mark didn't bother. After his accident, his wife couldn't access his accounts. She had to drag herself to court for months just to pay the mortgage. Thousands of dollars in legal fees, endless stress, all preventable.

**The Medical Showdown**
James knew his family couldn't agree on anything, so he named his best friend as medical POA. When he landed in the ICU, there was one voice in charge. His wishes were honored, no bickering in the waiting room, no lawsuits.

## Section Summary – Power of Attorney

> *Think of your POA as the bouncer at the door, keeping drama out and order in.*

Write down one person you trust with your finances if you were out cold.

_______________________________

_______________________________

_______________________________

Write down one person you trust with your medical care.

_______________________________

_______________________________

_______________________________

If they're different, perfect—you can split the job.

_______________________________

_______________________________

_______________________________

Bonus: actually ask them if they'll do it. Awkward now beats chaos later.

_______________________________

_______________________________

_______________________________

Use this space to write down what you discovered in this chapter and the actions you still need to take. List the people you're considering as your Power of Attorney, questions you need to ask, and where to find the right forms or notary.

This chapter was about **appointing your MVP—your Power of Attorney.** Choose who you trust to handle your life if you can't. Write their names, contact info, and backups. Then make it official so your finances, health, and sanity stay protected no matter what curveballs life throws your way.

# WHO CARES? — LONG-TERM CARE & WHO SHOWS UP WHEN YOU CAN'T

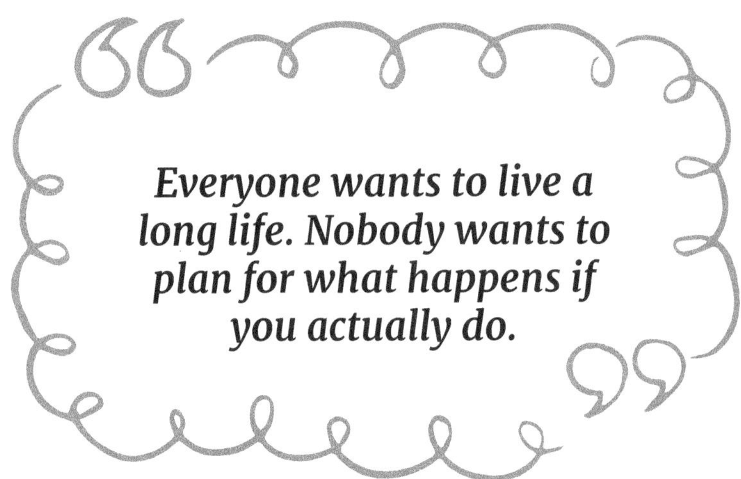


## *(a.k.a. Planning Before the Crisis Hits)*

Let's get real: most of us picture old age like a glossy retirement brochure — sipping wine in Tuscany, teaching grandkids to fish, maybe taking that wine and paint class you swore you'd try someday. What we don't picture? Slipping in the shower, breaking a hip, and suddenly needing help just to put on socks. But the truth is, living longer often comes with a price — and it's not just the one on the medical bill.

Here's the thing about long-term care: it's not just about nursing homes or "ending up somewhere." It's about who shows up when you can't. If you don't plan ahead, your family becomes the default plan. Your daughter quits her job. Your son gets burned out managing your meds between work and his own kids. Everyone's exhausted, broke, and quietly

resentful — all while trying to love you through it. Sound harsh? It's reality for millions of families every year.

Long-term care isn't just medical — it's emotional, physical, and financial. Whether it's in-home caregivers, assisted living, or a skilled nursing facility, it takes coordination, money, and tough conversations. And what most of us don't realize is that the earlier you plan, the more options you have. Wait until crisis mode hits, and you're stuck with whatever's available — and whatever's left in your savings account.

Many people avoid this topic because it's uncomfortable. Nobody wants to imagine themselves frail and asking for help buttoning their shirt. But pretending it won't happen doesn't protect you — it just dumps the problem on someone else. And that "someone else" is usually the closest to you.

Planning now means deciding what you want before life decides for you. Do you want to age at home? Hire a caregiver? Move into an active community with social events and a wine club? How will you pay for it — long-term care insurance, savings, or selling the house you no longer need? These aren't depressing questions. They're realistic, empowering ones. Because the real power move isn't avoiding the future — it's shaping it with your decisions.

Think of it this way: this isn't about giving up control. It's about keeping it. You get to design your own backup plan. You get to say who's in charge, where you live, how you're cared for, and what quality of life looks like to you. So when the time comes — whether it's a temporary recovery or a long road ahead — you're not a burden, you're prepared.

Because the truth is, long life isn't the goal — good life is. And good life, right up until the end, starts with a plan.

# The Realities of Caregiving

**70% of adults over 65** will need some kind of long-term care before they die.

The average cost of a private nursing home room? Over **$100,000 a year.**

And get this: Medicare doesn't cover "custodial care" (help with daily activities like bathing, eating, or dressing).

So unless you have a plan, your loved ones may become your default caregivers. Which sounds sweet... until you realize your adult child is working full-time, raising kids of their own, and now trying to juggle your meds, meals, and medical bills. Burnout is real. And resentment will replace tenderness very quickly.

## Your Options
## (a.k.a. Pick Your Long Term Adventure)

### Stay at Home With Help

- In-home care aides, visiting nurses, or family support.

- Pro: You're comfortable at home.

- Con: Can get pricey, especially 24/7 care.

### Assisted Living

- Independent-ish living with meals, activities, and support.

- Pro: Social, less lonely, lighter caregiving load.

- Con: Still thousands per month.

### Nursing Home / Skilled Care

- Full medical support for serious needs.

- Pro: Highest level of care.

- Con: Eye-watering cost, and not always your vibe.

### Hybrid & Family Caregiving

- A mix of adult day programs, respite care, and family pitching in.

- Pro: Flexible, cheaper.

- Con: Family burnout risk.

### The Money Side

This is where most people choke. Long-term care isn't cheap, and it doesn't magically pay for itself. Here are your main funding tools:

- Long-Term Care Insurance – Buy it before you're old. Gets more expensive (and harder to qualify for) every year you wait.

- Hybrid Life + Care Policies – Life insurance that doubles as long-term care coverage.

- Savings & Investments – Earmark funds specifically for future care.

Medicaid – Only kicks in if you basically spend down your assets first. Not the glamorous option, but it's a safety net.

Family Planning – Sometimes the "fund" is your kids. If that's your plan, at least be honest about it with them so they can prepare.

**The Human Side**

It's not just about money. It's about dignity, family dynamics, and clarity. Ask yourself:
Do I want to stay at home as long as possible?

Am I okay with assisted living if it's the right fit?

Who in my family would I trust to step in—and do they even know that's my expectation?

Keep in mind, if you don't have these conversations, your family will guess. And guessing is where the emotional landmines start. One child steps up and burns out while another stays on the sidelines and feels guilty. Resentment brews. Old sibling rivalries suddenly wake from the dead. What begins as "we're just trying to help Mom" turns into whispered phone calls, quiet scorekeeping, and someone inevitably muttering, "I'm the only one who does anything around here."

It's not that your family doesn't love you — it's that love doesn't automatically come with a game plan. When people are forced to make decisions in crisis, emotions run high and logic runs out the door. The best gift you can give them is clarity. A plan. A conversation that says, *"Here's what I want, here's how I want to live, and here's how I've prepared for it."*

When everyone knows the plan, there's less confusion, fewer fights, and a whole lot more compassion. Instead of arguing about who's doing more, your loved ones can focus on what actually matters — being there for you, not battling each other over the logistics of your care.

## Real-Life Stories

- **The Silent Sacrifice** – Maria moved in with her mom "just for a year." Ten years later, her own health had tanked from stress. She said the hardest part wasn't the care—it was that nobody had planned for it.

- **The Planner** – Jim bought long-term care insurance in his fifties. When Parkinson's hit, his wife never had to drain their savings. She said it was the best financial decision they ever made.

- **The Surprise** – After a fall, Harold needed care fast. No plan, no insurance. His kids scrambled to cover bills, took turns caring for him, and nearly lost their jobs in the process.

  - **Lesson:** Caregiving happens. It's that simple. Planning for it keeps love from turning into burnout.

## Section Summary – Long-Term Care

Don't leave your future up to chance—or your family's Google search history for 'cheap nursing homes near me.'"

## Mini Homework Prompt:

Write down your honest answers to these three:

- Would you rather stay home, even if it costs more, or move into assisted living when the time comes?

_______________________________________

_______________________________________

_______________________________________

_______________________________________

- If you had the option for family to care for you, who would you choose to be with?

_______________________________________

_______________________________________

_______________________________________

_______________________________________

- Do you want your family directly providing care—or just managing it?

_______________________________________

_______________________________________

_______________________________________

- What money (or insurance) is in place to make that choice possible?

---

---

---

If you don't have a financial plan for this today, it's time to get busy making a plan.

Use this space to jot down your thoughts, decisions, and next steps from this chapter. Write out questions for your doctor or insurance provider, potential facilities or caregivers to research, and any family conversations you need to start.

This chapter was about **long-term care—and who actually shows up when you can't**. Note your preferences for where and how you want to be cared for, the people you trust to advocate for you, and any coverage or plans you still need to secure. Planning now means comfort, dignity, and fewer crises later.

# CHAPTER 8

# FOLLOW THE MONEY

## (a.k.a. What Really Happens to Your Bills When You're Dead)

Ah yes, bills. The uninvited guest that never leaves. They show up monthly, eat your paycheck, and somehow multiply when you're not looking—like rabbits in mating season. They don't care if you're sick, tired, or soul-weary from just getting by they'll still knock on your door right on schedule, smiling like they own the place.

It's funny how we spend so much of our lives juggling them—mortgage, car, insurance, subscriptions we forgot we signed up for—half convinced that someday, maybe after a raise or a miracle, we'll finally get ahead. And plenty of people joke that the only real way to escape debt is by dying. Well guess what? Death does not come with a total debt eraser. (If only.)

Contrary to how life might feel on those nights when you open your banking app with one eye closed—you weren't born just to pay bills and die. You were meant to live, to laugh, to do something meaningful in between all those due dates. But the truth is, when your time is up, those bills don't evaporate into a puff of fairy dust. They hang around like unwanted party guests, waiting to see who's picking up the tab.

What happens next depends on the type of debt, where you live, and whether you were smart enough to make a plan. A solid one. Because the difference between leaving your loved ones a smooth transition and leaving them knee-deep in financial chaos often comes down to what you put in writing now. So yes, let's talk about the unsexy, unavoidable, utterly important topic of what happens to your money—and your avoidable mess—after you're gone.

## The Truth About Debt After Death

Here's where things get interesting — and slightly depressing. When you die, your debts don't die with you. Nope. They hang around like nosy relatives at Thanksgiving. And just when you think you've finally escaped your mortgage, car payment, or that Amazon haul from 2021 that you charged, guess what? The system has other plans.

According to the Consumer Financial Protection Bureau, when you pass away your debts get paid out of your estate. Translation: before your kids get a penny, the mortgage company, Visa, and the hospital all get their slice. It's like a final round of musical chairs — and the creditors always get the first seat.

If your estate has assets: Debts are paid first, then your heirs get what's left.

**If your estate is broke:** Creditors may just be out of luck. (Unless you happen to live in a community property state — where 'what's yours is mine' doesn't stop, even after death.)

**If you're married in AZ, CA, ID, LA, NV, NM, TX, WA, WI:** Congrats, your spouse may inherit your debt whether they want it or not. Till death not debt do you part.



## What Dies With You vs. What Sticks Around

**Usually Discharged (poof, gone):**

- Federal student loans – wiped out when you die. (Parent PLUS loans too.)

- Personal credit cards in your name only – balance paid/ written off from your estate.

**Usually Stick Around (sorry):**

- Mortgages – whoever gets the house also gets the debt. Surprise!

- Car loans – same deal. The car = the loan.

- Medical bills – those fun little surprises often hit your estate.

**Special Cases (aka, the fine print nobody reads):**

- Co-signers: If your mom co-signed that car loan in 1998, guess what—she's still on the hook when you're gone if you still have a balance.

- Joint accounts: The survivor is responsible, period.

Community property states: Spouses may be responsible for anything taken on during the marriage, even if they didn't know about it.

Silver lining: debt collectors can't harass your family into paying bills they don't owe. They can contact your estate, but they can't guilt-trip your spouse into Venmo-ing them.

## Why Budgeting Now Matters (Yes, While You're Alive)

Here's the part you don't want to hear: if you don't know where your money is going, your family sure won't. And grief + mystery bills = disaster.

Ask yourself:

Do I know my exact credit card balances?

Do I know which bills are on autopay and which aren't?

Does anyone else know how to log into my mortgage account?

If you're shrugging, imagine your executor (probably your spouse or kid, already crying) trying to guess your screen password where all the other secret passwords are hiding, while also dealing with your funeral. You don't want this to be your last memory.

Budgeting now isn't about skipping your favorite frappuccino every day. It's about making sure your loved ones don't have to play a game of financial hide-and-seek when you're gone.

## Gather the Receipts (Literally)

There's no one "right" way to organize. Spreadsheet, binder, shoebox, post-its—do whatever you'll actually keep up with. Just start.

Collect:

## Section 1: Monthly bills (utilities, phone, etc.)

#1 Name of Payee/Company________________________________

User name/Email________________________________

Account Number________________________________

Account log in site________________________________

Password________________________________

Notes________________________________

#2 Name of Payee/Company________________________________

User name/Email________________________________

Account Number________________________________

Account log in site________________________________

Password________________________________

Notes________________________________

#3 Name of Payee/Company________________________________

User name/Email________________________________

Account Number________________________________

Account log in site________________________________

Password________________________________

Notes________________________________

#4 Name of Payee/Company______________________________________

User name/Email______________________________________

Account Number______________________________________

Account log in site______________________________________

Password______________________________________

Notes______________________________________

## Section 2: Credit cards + balances

#1 Name of Payee/Credit Card Company______________________

User name/Email______________________________________

Account Number______________________________________

Account log in site______________________________________

Password______________________________________

Notes ______________________________________

#2 Name of Payee/Credit Card Company______________________

User name/Email______________________________________

Account Number______________________________________

Account log in site______________________________________

Password______________________________________

Notes ______________________________________

#3 Name of Payee/Credit Card Company_______________________

User name/Email_____________________________________

Account Number_____________________________________

Account log in site___________________________________

Password___________________________________________

Notes _______________________________________________


#4 Name of Payee/Credit Card Company_______________________

User name/Email_____________________________________

Account Number_____________________________________

Account log in site___________________________________

Password___________________________________________

Notes _______________________________________________

#5 Name of Payee/Credit Card Company_______________________

User name/Email_____________________________________

Account Number_____________________________________

Account log in site___________________________________

Password___________________________________________

Notes _______________________________________________

## Section 3: Bank Information for loans, car payments, student loans, etc.

#1 Name of Bank/Payee Contact info________________________

User name/Email________________________

Account Number________________________

Password________________________

Notes________________________

#2 Name of Bank/Payee Contact info________________________

User name/Email________________________

Account Number________________________

Password________________________

Notes________________________

#3 Name of Bank/Payee Contact info________________________

User name/Email________________________

Account Number________________________

Password________________________

Notes________________________

#4 Name of Bank/Payee Contact info________________________

User name/Email________________________

Account Number________________________

Password________________________

Notes________________________

#5 Name of Bank/Payee Contact info_____________________________

User name/Email_____________________________________________

Account Number______________________________________________

Password___________________________________________________

Notes_______________________________________________________

## Section 4: Mortgage Details

#1 Name of Mortgage Loan Bank/Payee Contact info

_____________________________________________________________

User name/Email_____________________________________________

Account Number______________________________________________

Account log in site__________________________________________

Password___________________________________________________

Notes ______________________________________________________

#2 Name of Mortgage Loan Bank/Payee Contact info

_____________________________________________________________

User name/Email_____________________________________________

Account Number______________________________________________

Account log in site__________________________________________

Password___________________________________________________

Notes ______________________________________________________

**Bonus points:** add user names, passwords, websites, account reps. The goal: someone you trust should be able to step in and run the show without having it turn into a Sherlock Holmes episode.

## Mini Homework Prompt:

- Write down your 5 biggest bills (mortgage/rent, car, utilities, credit card, loan).

_______________________________________

_______________________________________

_______________________________________

_______________________________________

_______________________________________

- Next to each, note: who's responsible if you die (estate, co-signer, joint account holder)? Go ahead, check the list above—we made it easy for you.

_______________________________________

_______________________________________

_______________________________________

- Start a binder/folder/spreadsheet with just those five. Then keep adding to it.

_______________________________________

_______________________________________

**The Mortgage Surprise**
Carla inherited her dad's house—and his $200k mortgage. She thought she was getting a free house. Instead, she had to sell it in six months because she couldn't pay the mortgage and taxes and couldn't find a buyer.

**The Credit Card Relief**
Mike died with $18k in credit card debt. His daughter panicked until she learned: it was in his name only, and his estate had nothing. Poof—gone. Huge relief.

**The Co-Signer Curse**
David co-signed his brother's car loan. When his brother passed, the bank came for David. He had no choice but to pay it off.

**Bottom line:** debt doesn't disappear—it just plays by its own rules. Know the rules, and plan ahead.

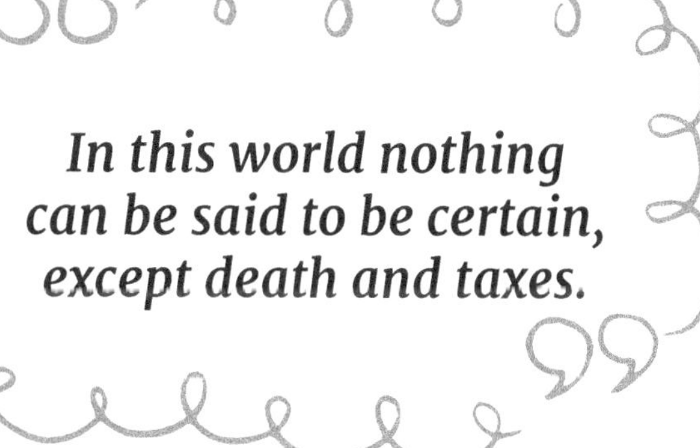


Here's the deal: when you die, the IRS doesn't just shrug and walk away. Somebody still has to handle your last round of paperwork.

**Final Income Tax Return**

- Your executor files your last personal tax return, covering income earned up until the day you die.

- Example: You pass away in July → your executor files a return the following April, just like always.

### Estate Taxes

- Federal estate tax only kicks in for very large estates (over $13.99 million as of 2025). Most people will never hit it.

- Some states, though, have their own estate or inheritance taxes with much lower thresholds. (Translation: even a modest estate might owe.)

### Inheritance Taxes

- A handful of states tax the people who inherit, not the estate itself. Sometimes spouses and kids are exempt, but not always (Do your homework.)

### Unpaid Taxes from the Past

- Owe back taxes? The IRS will still want them out of your estate before heirs see a dime.

Bottom line: your executor becomes the point person. If you don't leave them organized records, they'll be piecing things together while trying to grieve. This is probably not the legacy you have in mind.

## Real Life Example

When Susan's dad died, she found out he hadn't filed taxes for the past two years. Sorting it out took months, cost thousands in accountant fees, and delayed closing the estate. The inheritance wasn't huge, but the stress was.

Lesson: even if your estate is small, your tax paperwork matters. Leave it as tidy as that fancy Air BNB when you first check in.

## Quick Prep Checklist

△ Keep copies of your last 3 years of tax returns in your designated "important docs" folder.

△ If you live in a state with inheritance/estate taxes, note it clearly for your executor.

△ List your CPA or tax preparer's contact info (if you use one).

CPA Contact information:  ___________________________

ACCOUNTANT Contact info:  ___________________________

# Bills & Debts Worksheet

*(Organize What You Owe and Who's Responsible)*

## Section 1: Monthly Bills

| Bills/ Service | Amount | Due Date | Website/login | Notes |
|---|---|---|---|---|
| | | | | |
| | | | | |
| | | | | |
| | | | | |
| | | | | |
| | | | | |

## Section 2: Mortgage Details

| Type(Mortgage/ Car/Personal) | Balance | Payment | Co-Signature/ Joint | Notes |
|---|---|---|---|---|
| | | | | |
| | | | | |
| | | | | |
| | | | | |
| | | | | |
| | | | | |

## Section 3: Credit Cards

| Issuer | Balance | Payment Due | Joint or Authorized User | Notes |
|---|---|---|---|---|
|  |  |  |  |  |
|  |  |  |  |  |
|  |  |  |  |  |
|  |  |  |  |  |
|  |  |  |  |  |
|  |  |  |  |  |

## Section 4: Medical Bills and Other Bills

| Type | Balance | Due Date | Notes |
|---|---|---|---|
|  |  |  |  |
|  |  |  |  |
|  |  |  |  |
|  |  |  |  |
|  |  |  |  |
|  |  |  |  |

Use this section to note what you learned and what you still need to tackle. Write down your accounts, debts, and automatic payments. Make a list of who needs access, what needs to be canceled, and any balances or due dates to double-check.

This chapter was about **following the money—who pays your bills when you're gone.** Get clear on what's owed, what disappears, and what keeps ticking after you're not here to manage it. The goal: no mystery bills, no financial chaos, and no family detective work required.

_______________________________________________

_______________________________________________

_______________________________________________

_______________________________________________

_______________________________________________

_______________________________________________

_______________________________________________

_______________________________________________

_______________________________________________

# CHAPTER 9

# GIVING IT AWAY BEFORE YOU GO

> *Don't let your treasures turn into tomorrow's estate sale.*

## *(a.k.a. How to Share the Wealth Without Starting a Family Brawl)*

Let's be honest—waiting until you die to pass things on is overrated. Sure, wills and trusts handle the leftovers, but why let your best stuff sit in a box until you're gone? Giving while you're alive is the ultimate power move. You get to see the joy, the gratitude, the eye-rolls, and sometimes even the happy tears. You get to tell the story behind each gift instead of having people guess later. ("Why did Grandma leave *me* the cuckoo clock?")

Think of it this way: giving now turns your "estate" into something alive, something that connects you to the people and causes you care about. You get to *witness* your generosity doing what it's meant to do — changing someone's day, or even their life. Maybe it's helping your granddaughter with her first apartment deposit. Maybe it's donating to an animal shelter that always makes you tear up. Maybe it's giving your best friend that heirloom bracelet because she's the one who always admired it. Big or small, giving now makes the story richer.

And let's be real — this isn't just about warm, fuzzy feelings. It's also strategic. Giving now can help reduce estate taxes, simplify probate later, and prevent your kids from reenacting a scene from *The Hunger Games* over who gets the china cabinet. When you make the decisions yourself, you take the fight out of their hands. Plus, you get the bonus of seeing your things loved, used, and appreciated instead of collecting dust or sparking drama.

"Stuff" carries energy — memories, emotions, moments in time. When you choose who gets what, you're also choosing the legacy that goes with it. You get to tell your kids *why* that recipe box matters, or what that painting meant to you. That context turns ordinary objects into keepsakes instead of clutter.

And let's not forget charitable giving. You don't have to be a millionaire to make a difference. You don't need a foundation with your name on it or a bronze plaque outside a hospital. Maybe you sponsor a student, plant trees, fund a community project, or make a donation to a cause that aligns with your heart. The beauty of giving while you're still around is that you get to see the ripple effect. You get to witness your money—or your time, or your wisdom—turn into something that lasts.

In the end, giving now isn't about letting go—it's about letting in. Letting in joy, gratitude, and connection. It's about seeing what your legacy looks like while you're still here to enjoy it. Because let's face it: the best part of generosity isn't the giving itself—it's watching what happens next.

## Why Give it Away While You're Alive?

**You get to see the impact.** Whether it's your granddaughter's college tuition or a local shelter that buys new beds because of your donation, you're here to witness the good.

**You control the story.** Instead of your family arguing over who gets what, you decide — in person.

**You may save money.** Strategic gifting can lower estate taxes or even qualify you for tax breaks.

Translation: you don't have to be Warren Buffet to make this work. Even modest giving can change the story your family remembers.

> *Leave something behind that can't be taxed, sold, or divided -a little good in the world.*

You don't need to start a foundation with your name carved into a marble plaque or a library wing dedicated in your honor. Legacy doesn't have to come with a tax ID number or a black tie gala with a plated dinner for $500. Giving can be as simple or as grand as you want it to be — the size doesn't matter, the heart behind it does. What matters is that it reflects your values and the kind of ripple you want to leave in the world.

Maybe it's funding a scholarship for kids who remind you of your younger self. It could be donating your books to the local library, your instruments to a music program, or setting aside something for a cause that shaped your own life.

Your impact doesn't have to shout; sometimes it's a quiet gesture that keeps echoing long after you're gone. Options include:

- **One-Time Donations** – Pick your favorite cause and support it now.

- **Recurring Giving** – Monthly donations to a church, nonprofit, or cause close to your heart.

- **Donor-Advised Funds (DAFs)** – A "giving account" where you set money aside now, get a tax deduction, and direct the funds later.

- **Charitable Bequests** – Name a charity in your will. Easy way to leave a legacy.

- **Scholarships or Endowments** – Create something lasting in your name (or anonymously, if you're low-key).

**Pro tip:** If you've got a charity you love, tell your family why. When they understand the story behind your giving, they'll honor it instead of questioning it.

### Family Gifting: Passing the Baton

When it comes to family, giving isn't always about cash. It's about easing the future and creating meaning now.

- **Annual Gift Exclusion** – You can give up to a certain amount (check the yearly IRS limit, often around $19k* per person (as of 2025), depending on annual adjustments) without gift tax. Perfect for spreading the love.

- **Education & Medical** – Pay tuition or medical bills directly — it doesn't even count toward that limit.

- **Property Transfers** – Passing a house, car, or cabin while you're alive (but beware of tax implications).

- **Heirlooms & Sentimental Stuff** – Don't wait until they're fighting at your funeral. Hand it over now, with the story that makes it priceless.

Giving doesn't have to mean equal — but it should be intentional. If you're giving one kid the piano and another the photo albums, explain why. Silence creates resentment; stories create understanding.

### The Emotional Side

Money is one thing, but meaning is another. Giving can also be:

- **Traditions** – Teaching a grandchild how to cook your holiday dish.

- **Stories** – Writing down the history behind a keepsake.

- **Time** – Showing up, listening, mentoring.

- **Blessings** – Saying, out loud, what each person means to you.

These "gifts" often outlive the stuff. A note tucked inside a recipe book might mean more than the diamond ring.

## Real Life Stories

The Peaceful Planner – Elaine gifted her jewelry to her daughters while she was alive, each with a handwritten note. On the day of her funeral, there were no fights — just shared laughter about the stories behind each piece.

The Tax-Smart Grandpa – Dan set up a donor-advised fund in his 70s. Every Christmas, his grandkids helped pick which charities to support. It became a family tradition and taught them generosity firsthand.

The Missed Chance – Frank kept saying he'd "leave something for the church." He never wrote it down, and when his estate went through probate, nothing made it there. His family felt guilty — and the church missed the help.

- Lesson: giving works best when it's written, clear, and done with love.

**Section Summary – Giving It Away Before You Go**

- Giving while alive = joy, control, and sometimes tax savings.

- Charitable options: one-time gifts, monthly donations, donor-advised funds, scholarships.

- Family gifts: annual cash, tuition/medical, property, heirlooms.

- Explain the *why* — meaning matters more than money.

Write down:

- One charity or cause you'd love to support (now or later).

_______________________________________________

_______________________________________________

- One family member or friend you want to gift something meaningful to while you're alive.

_________________________________________

_________________________________________

- One heirloom or tradition you'd like to hand over with a story.

_________________________________________

_________________________________________

Start small. Write it, share it, and let them know it matters.

## 📝 Notes & Next Steps

Use this space to jot down what you discovered in this chapter—who you want to bless with your treasures, what needs organizing, and which causes or charities you want to support. Make a list of gifts to give now, items to pass down later, and any donations or legacy contributions you'd like to set up.

This chapter was about giving it away before you go—sharing your treasures and your generosity while you're here to witness the impact. Whether it's family, friends, or a cause close to your heart, note where you want your time, money, and memories to go. The goal: less stuff collecting dust, more goodness paying forward.

# CHAPTER 10

# LAST WILL & TESTAMENT: WHO GETS WHAT (AND WHO DOESN'T)

> *Where there's a will...*
> *there's a family*
> *argument waiting to*
> *happen.*

## *(a.k.a. Your Final Plot Twist)*

Let's cut to the chase: everyone needs a will. Yes, even you. I don't care if you don't own a yacht, a vacation home, or a closet full of Fendi bags. A will isn't some fancy legal luxury reserved for people with private jets and family lawyers—it's for anyone who owns anything, or loves anyone and wants to keep them from arguing when you're gone.

Because here's how it really works: If you don't have a will, the state decides what happens next. And the state doesn't know Jack about your family drama. They don't care that cousin Eddie still owes you money, that your sister hasn't spoken to you since the *Great Thanksgiving Incident of 2014*, or that your ex is one bad day away from pawning your vinyl collection. The state just follows a routine formula called *intestate succession*—and your estate will be divided up like leftover Halloween candy: sadly, unevenly, and definitely not how you pictured it.

A will is your voice from beyond the grave—your PSA that says, "Here's how this goes." Without it, you're leaving your loved ones to play an expensive, emotionally charged guessing game that could drag on for years. With it, you're giving them peace, clarity, and maybe a few surprises.

Think of it as your final act. You've spent a lifetime collecting memories, building relationships, and accumulating stuff that—let's be honest—means more to you than its actual price tag. A will lets you tie all of that together into one last parting message. You get to decide who gets the heirloom jewelry, the dog, the family recipes, and yes, even your Stanley collection. You also get to ensure that nobody swoops in to "call dibs" on something you never wanted them to have in the first place.

And here's the thing—writing a will isn't morbid. It's liberating. It's saying, *I'm still the author of my story, even after the credits roll.* A good will doesn't just divide assets—it protects relationships, closes loops, and gives your people one final gift: direction in the middle of chaos.

Because in the end, your life isn't just about the things you leave behind—it's about the thoughtfulness with which you leave them.

## What a Will Actually Does (Your Posthumous Megaphone)

A will is your chance to call the shots one last time:

- **Who gets what.** The house, the car, the savings, grandma's pearls, your 8 track collection, the dusty recliner in the basement that everyone hated.

- **Who's in charge.** You appoint an executor to run the show. (Think project manager, but for getting shit done.)

- **Who gets the kids.** If you have minors, this is where you name a guardian. Don't leave it to chance. If you think people were fighting over your watch collection, wait till you see two grandmas go at it over the grandkids.

- **Who doesn't get a damn thing.** (Yes, this is a touchy but very real subject.) Want to make sure your freeloading cousin or deadbeat sibling gets zero? A will makes it official.

- **Charities & causes.** Want to leave money to a shelter, church, or your favorite wiener dog bingo fundraiser? A will makes sure it happens.

- **Sidenote:** Retirement accounts and pensions don't play by the same rules as your will. Whoever you listed as the beneficiary 20 years ago? If you haven't changed it, they're still first in line... even if you divorced them, remarried, and started a whole new family. So check those forms now! Don't let your ex walk off with your hard-earned retirement while your current spouse gets nothing but the wilted houseplants.

## What a Will Doesn't Do (Don't Get It Twisted)

- **It doesn't override assets with named beneficiaries.** (Life insurance, retirement accounts, joint bank accounts — those go straight to whoever's listed, no matter what your will says.) Even more of a reason to circle back and check whose name you listed as beneficiary. (This is good reminder to go back and review Chapter 5: The Surprise Beneficiary.)

- It doesn't skip probate. Your will still has to be validated in court.

It doesn't cover what happens if you're alive but incapacitated. That's what powers of attorney and advance directives are for. Is this starting to make sense?

## Will vs. Trust: The Showdown

| Will: | Trust: |
|---|---|
| Basic. Cheap. Everyone should have one. Kicks in when you die. Goes through probate (the dreaded red-tape circus). | Fancier. Holds your assets while you're alive, avoids probate, and gives you more control. Costs more, but way more private. |

### So what exactly is Probate?

Probate is the official court process that kicks in after someone dies to prove their will is valid, pay off any debts, and then distribute whatever's left to the rightful heirs. Think of it as the referee of the estate game — the court makes sure everything is handled by the rules. Sounds orderly, but here's the catch: probate can be slow, public, and expensive. Depending on the state and the size of the estate, it can drag on for months (sometimes years), with court fees and lawyer costs eating into what's left. That's why so many people look for ways to simplify or avoid probate when possible — trusts, joint ownership, and named beneficiaries can all keep assets out of the hands of The People's Court.

**Translation:** For most people, a will is the bare minimum. If you've got major assets or just hate the idea of lawyers sniffing through your stuff, a trust might be the way to go.

# Common Will Mistakes
# (a.k.a. Don't Be This Person)

- **Not writing one at all.** The #1 mistake.

- **Never updating it.** Divorce, remarriage, new kids, new house — your will needs a refresh like your phone apps, your haircut, and your wardrobe.

- **Being vague.** "I leave my stuff to my kids." Congratulations, you just started World War III.

- **Forgetting backups.** Executors die, guardians move, life happens. Always name alternates.

- **DIY disasters.** A will on a cocktail napkin can be legal in some states, but it's about as valid as the lipstick stain on the corner of it.

## Real Life Stories: With vs. Without

**The Smooth Transfer**
Linda had a simple will. Her daughter was executor, her three kids split everything evenly. No drama, no fights, just closure. The family stayed close.

**The Surprise Twist**
Terry thought he had everything handled. He'd updated his will, appointed an executor, even set up a trust. What he didn't update? The beneficiary on his life insurance policy from a job he left twenty years ago. When he died, the payout—six figures—went straight to his ex-girlfriend from the 90s. His current wife was blindsided, his kids were heartbroken, and the ex? She cashed the check. One small oversight, one massive fallout.

Moral of the story: A plan is only as good as its last update.

## The Probate Nightmare

Ben died without a will. Two kids from marriage #1, a current wife, zero instructions. The state split his estate in a way that left everyone angry. Court battles dragged on for years. His family tree? Basically scorched like a wild fire with little chance for regrowth.

- Lesson: a will is not just about dividing your stuff. It's about preventing chaos and giving your family peace (or at least direction).

## Section Summary – Wills

- A will = your voice after death.
- It covers who gets what, who's in charge, and who raises your kids.
- It doesn't override beneficiaries or avoid probate.
- Trusts = more control, more privacy, more money left behind.
- Avoid these mistakes: no will, no updates, vague instructions, no backups.
- Bottom line: write it, update it, and actually share it.

## Mini homework assignment:

- Contact information of attorney used for your will or trust

______________________________________________

- Date of most recent version completed:

______________________________________________

- Location copy is stored:

___________________________________________



Start with the basics. Take stock of your assets. All of them—from bank accounts to crypto accounts to dirt bikes and rare stamp collections. It's time to be as responsible with your worldly goods before you become... unworldly.

Next, do a little soul searching. Who might make the cut as your executor? Who would you want to care for your children or pets? What are those most important possessions you want passed to that special someone that would really value and appreciate them like you do?

Since part of the will-trust-probate equation is distributing assets and paying off your debts, take time to complete the charts below to ensure a smoother transition.

- List options for your executor (your post-life project manager).

___________________________________________

___________________________________________

- List guardians who you'd want to care for your kids (if you have them).

___________________________________________

___________________________________________

- List your top 5 assets and who should inherit them.

________________________________________

________________________________________

________________________________________

________________________________________

- List any other personal items of sentimental value that you want specific people to have.

________________________________________

________________________________________

________________________________________

________________________________________

Bonus: set a reminder to revisit this list every 2 years or after any major life change (marriage, divorce, new baby, lottery win, health speed bump, etc.).

# Will Worksheet

*(Your "who gets what" Cheat Sheet)*

### Section 1: Executor

| | |
|---|---|
| Executor Name: | |
| Relationship: | |
| Backup Executor Name: | |
| Relationship: | |

## Section 2: Guardians for Minor Children

| | |
|---|---|
| Guardian Name: | |
| Relationship: | |
| Backup Guardian Name: | |
| Relationship: | |

## Section 3: Key Assets & Beneficiaries

| Asset | Beneficiary | Notes |
|---|---|---|
| | | |
| | | |
| | | |
| | | |
| | | |
| | | |

## Section 4: Special Gifts or Instructions

| Items/Instruction | Beneficiary | Notes |
|---|---|---|
| | | |
| | | |
| | | |
| | | |

## Section 5: Charities or Organizations

| Charity/Org | Gift/Amount | Notes |
|---|---|---|
| | | |
| | | |
| | | |
| | | |

# Personal Property Distribution Worksheet

*(Jewelry, Collections, Heirlooms, and Special Items)*

List out items of personal value and who should receive them. Be as specific as possible (e.g., 'Grandma's wedding ring' instead of just 'jewelry').

| Item Description | Beneficiary | Location of Item | Notes |
|---|---|---|---|
|  |  |  |  |
|  |  |  |  |
|  |  |  |  |
|  |  |  |  |
|  |  |  |  |
|  |  |  |  |
|  |  |  |  |
|  |  |  |  |
|  |  |  |  |
|  |  |  |  |

Use this space to record what you learned in this chapter—who gets what, who's in charge, and what still needs to be written or updated. Jot down your executor's name, potential guardians, and any assets or accounts you need to include in your will.

This chapter was about your Last Will and Testament—your final say in who gets what (and who doesn't). Note

the updates to make, beneficiaries to double-check, and professionals you would contact for legal help if needed. The goal: no confusion, no courtroom drama, and a clear plan that reflects your true intentions.

# CHAPTER 11

# WHILE YOU'RE HERE...

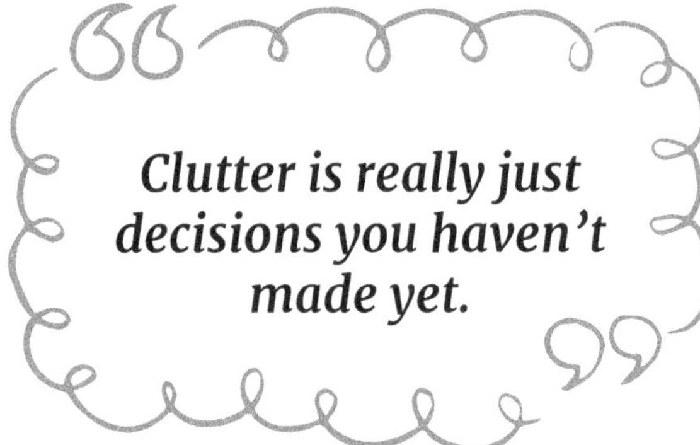


## *(a.k.a. Don't Leave Your Family Knee-Deep in Your Junk Drawer)*

Let's be real: most of us aren't exactly spring-cleaning through life on a daily basis. We've got boxes in the garage labeled *"misc,"* drawers that could qualify as archeological digs, and kitchen gadgets we haven't touched since Jesus was a baby. Somewhere in the back of a closet, there's probably a half-finished scrapbook, three broken picture frames, and a mystery cord that must go to something important— right? We keep it all because "someday" we'll deal with it. Someday, when life slows down. Someday, when we finally get organized. The reality is: someday rarely comes.

And while you might shrug and think, *meh, they can deal with it when I'm gone,* the truth is—your family will be grieving. And sorting through decades of clutter isn't therapeutic when your heart's broken; it's torture. It's not "going through Mom's things," it's hours of confusion, guilt, and wondering what mattered enough to keep. Every old receipt, every unlabeled photo, every "just in case" box becomes an emotional landmine.

That's where **While You're Here Tips** comes in. Think of it as kindness disguised as organization—a love letter written in labeled bins and neatly stacked papers. It's not glamorous, but it's the difference between your kids sitting on the floor, laughing together while flipping through your photo albums, versus cursing your name as they haul 16 garbage bags of "someday craft projects" to Goodwill.

It's also a moment of clarity for *you.* Cleaning up your physical life helps clean up your mental one. You will see what you've held on to, what still matters, and what can finally go. You give yourself the chance to shape your own story, rather than letting someone else dig through the leftovers of it.

In short—it's not just about leaving less for others to sort through. It's about living with more intention, right now.

## The Great Declutter

We all have more stuff than we need. That's just modern life — a mix of nostalgia, Amazon impulse buys, and "but it was on sale" moments that somehow multiply when we're not looking. Closets stuffed to the brim, garages packed tighter than an overstuffed suitcase on vacation, and enough random home décor to open a thrift shop of our own. But here's the question: do you *really* want your family arguing over which of your 27 Stanleys goes to which niece or nephew?

Picture it — your loved ones standing in your kitchen after the service, bleary-eyed, holding mismatched lids and slow cookers, fighting over who "deserves" the one with the fancy digital timer. It sounds ridiculous... because it is. Yet it happens every day. People will go to battle over the most random things — the set of chipped Christmas mugs you loved, the armchair no one sat in, the holiday dish that was always part of the family tradition.

The truth is, the stuff we collect becomes emotional currency after we're gone. Every item tells a story, and when those stories aren't clear, people try to assign their own meaning. That's when feelings get hurt, relationships fracture, and family group texts go silent.

So yes — maybe you've got 27 Stanleys. But this isn't about cold drinks. It's about deciding what actually matters while you still can. What pieces of your life carry meaning, and which ones are just taking up space? Getting honest about that now means your family won't have to play emotional roulette later. They'll know what mattered to you — and they'll have permission to laugh, love, and let go of the rest.

Start now:

- Sort your stuff. Keep, donate, toss. (And for everyone's sanity, please label the boxes.)

- Downsize sentimental things. You don't need 150 birthday cards from the '90s. Keep a few, let the rest go.

- Give heirlooms early. If you know who should have Grandma's quilt, hand it over now with the story attached. Watching them appreciate it while you're alive is a gift.

Think of this as editing your life before the final draft and then sitting back and enjoying the read.

## Downsizing Your Home

Downsizing isn't easy. I'll be the first to admit it. I went from raising a family of seven in a five-bedroom house with a pool and a garden into a small apartment that could practically fit inside my old living room. The first night felt strange—quiet in a way that didn't feel peaceful yet. Every box I unpacked came with a memory attached, and every piece of furniture made me second-guess what I was really ready to let go of.

Downsizing takes practicality, courage, and a lot of honesty with yourself. You're not just sorting through stuff—you're sorting through decades of life. It forces you to decide what's truly worth keeping and what's simply been along for the ride.

And to be honest, at some point, most of us are living in way more space than we actually use. The kids are grown, the upstairs hasn't been touched in years, and somehow you still have three bathrooms even though you only ever use one. So why heat, cool, and pay for a house that mostly holds memories and dust?

Downsizing isn't about giving up—it's about freeing up. Space. Energy. Money. Time. And maybe a little peace of mind too.

## *Why it makes sense:*

Downsizing makes sense for a lot of reasons—practical and emotional. A smaller space means smaller bills, less upkeep, and more time to actually enjoy your life instead of managing it. You're not giving up; you're streamlining. Fewer rooms to clean, fewer things to worry about, and more freedom to focus on what matters now—not the stuff you've been storing "just in case" for decades. It's about living lighter, not smaller.

Translation: downsizing isn't about shrinking your life. It's about creating the space, time, and money to live your best chapter yet.

## Photo + Memory Organization

Your shoeboxes of Polaroids? The random hard drive labeled "pics_final1989"? Those aren't clutter—they're time capsules. Each one holds a piece of your story, but unless you organize them, they'll just look like mystery piles to everyone else. Start by labeling what you can. A note like *"Mom, 1984, laughing at Dad's haircut"* is worth gold compared to a faded photo marked with three question marks and a Sharpie mark.

Then, take it a step further—digitize what you can. Scan the photos, upload the home videos, and save them somewhere your family can actually access (not on that old laptop you swore you'd fix one day). Cloud storage, an external drive, or even a shared family folder—just make sure someone knows how to find it.

But the real magic is in the stories. Add captions, notes, or voice recordings explaining who's who, what was happening, and why it mattered. I learned this once my husband passed away. I was left with no captions or hints. Just black and white pictures of people from the old country I couldn't identify for my children so the stories were lost for the next generation. "This was the day we got lost on the way to Grandma's and ended up at that weird roadside diner" will mean more than a thousand silent pictures ever could.

Because the truth is, your family doesn't just want the images—they want the context. They want the laughter behind the smiles, the stories behind the snapshots, and the memories told in your words. That's what keeps you alive in their hearts long after the ink fades.

- **Label them.** "Mom, 1984" is better than "???"

- **Digitize.** Scan photos, upload videos. Use cloud storage that your executor can actually access.

- **Tell the stories.** Add notes, captions, or even a quick voice recording so the meaning doesn't die with you.

**Everyday Logistics** Sometimes it's not the big legal documents that trip people up—it's the little things.

△ Everyday logistics—this is the stuff no one thinks to document until it's too late. It's not the legal papers or notarized signatures that cause the biggest headaches; it's the tiny, ordinary details of your daily life. The things so woven into your routine that you forget anyone else might need to know them.

△ Who has the spare house key? Where's the extra car key— the one you swear was in the junk drawer? What about the code for the garage door, or the alarm system that blows out your eardrums when you open the wrong door? Let's answer a few here:

Who has your spare house key?_______________________________________

Who has your spare car key?_________________________________________

Do you have a mailbox key and where do you keep it?

_____________________________________________________________________

How about extra garage door openers?_________________________

△ And then there are the living things—your pets and your plants. Who feeds the cat, knows which treats upset her stomach, or realizes that your dog won't sleep without his tattered penguin toy? Who's going to water the fiddle leaf fig you've nursed back from the brink twelve times already? (Because it won't survive on your good juju when you're gone.)

△ This is the heartbeat of your day-to-day life—the quiet background rhythm that makes everything flow. Without it, the people who love you will be standing in your kitchen, juggling keys, chasing your dog, and wondering why the houseplants are drooping while another subscription for "Bark Box" hits your credit card. Write it down. These little things may not feel important, but they're the map your family will need to find their way through the everyday chaos you kept running so effortlessly.

## Pre-Pay, Pre-Plan (Because Chaos Is Overrated)

If there's one universal truth about life (and death), it's that chaos loves an invitation. Pre-planning is how you politely decline. It's not glamorous, and it won't earn you a medal, but it *will* save your loved ones from a logistical circus at a time when they can barely remember to eat.

Start with the big one: **pre-paying funeral or cremation costs.** It might feel weird, but it's one of the kindest gifts you can leave behind. It removes an immediate financial burden and spares your family from sitting around a conference table at the funeral home, trying to make expensive decisions through tears and exhaustion. One less bill, one less argument, one less "Would they have wanted the deluxe urn or the wood box?"

Pre-planning doesn't make you morbid—it makes you merciful. You're clearing a path through the mess so your family doesn't have to. You're saying, "I've got this handled," even from beyond the paperwork. Because the truth is, chaos might make for great television, but in real life? It's wildly overrated.

# Real Life Stories

**The Chaos Closet** – When my husband died, my sister and I sat in my closet for 3 days pouring through stacks of papers that my pack rat husband left behind. He was brilliant, but he had a "paper problem." Every receipt, copy of bill, check, or anything that had a dollar sign on it, went into a pile... or another pile, or another pile. We were searching for anything that might hint at a banking password or login. Long story short—we never found it.

**The Thoughtful Dad** – Mark left a binder with labeled house keys, vet info, and even a list of where he kept spare batteries. His kids said it felt like he was still guiding them, even after he was gone.

**The Surprise Subscription** – One family discovered their dad had signed up for four streaming services and two wine clubs. The estate paid them for months before anyone noticed.

- Lesson: the little things matter just as much as the big ones.

## Baby Steps.

1. Pick one closet or drawer and start decluttering this week.
2. Write down the name of your pet's vet (or plant-watering instructions).
3. Make a quick list of your subscriptions and household services.
4. Bonus: Write down 3 pros and 3 cons of downsizing your home. Would it free you—or freak you out?

Use this space to capture your takeaways from this chapter—what to keep, what to donate, and what to finally toss. Make a list of areas to tackle (closets, garages, storage bins), people or charities to give items to, and any sentimental pieces that need labeling or stories attached.

This chapter was about decluttering—lightening your load while you still have a say in what stays and what goes. Simplify your space, make peace with your piles, and turn chaos into calm. The goal: less overwhelm for you now, and less mess for your loved ones later.

_________________________________________________

_________________________________________________

_________________________________________________

_________________________________________________

_________________________________________________

_________________________________________________

_________________________________________________

_________________________________________________

_________________________________________________

# CHAPTER 12

# WRITE YOUR OWN OBITUARY (OR AT LEAST HELP WITH THE DRAFT)

> *Live so fully that even your obituary makes people laugh and cry at the same time.*

## *(a.k.a. Don't Let Cousin Linda Reduce Your Life to Three Boring Paragraphs)*

Here's the truth: most obituaries are boring as hell. They're basically a list of jobs, dates, places, and surviving relatives, with maybe one line about "loved gardening and crossword puzzles." That might technically cover your life, but is that really how you want to be remembered?

Writing your own obituary (or at least sketching out your biography) isn't morbid — it's gaining a new perspective. It's like stepping outside yourself and seeing your life as others might tell it when you're gone. What stories would they include? What memories would they share? Would the highlight reel feel complete, or would there be glaring gaps where dreams got shelved and "somedays" never came?

When you write it yourself, you get to set the tone — warm, funny, heartfelt, or all three. You decide which quirks, milestones, and victories make the cut. But here's the real magic: you're not gone yet. You're still here, pen in hand, which means you get the rare gift of editing your story before the credits roll. If you don't like what you see on paper — too many should-haves, not enough I-dids — you've got time to change the plot. Add the trip, mend the relationship, start the project, chase the dream. Make sure your future self doesn't have to write around the regrets.

And yes, this still helps your family when the time comes. They won't be left crying, stressed, and piecing together a life story between casseroles and funeral potatoes. But more importantly, it helps you now — because nothing lights a fire under your "someday" list like reading your life as if it's already over.

## Why This Matters

- You own your story. Nobody knows your life better than you.

- It relieves stress. Your family won't be stuck Googling whether you graduated in '78 or '79.

- It's a gift. They get to celebrate your life, not stress about the wording.

- It's a reflection. Writing about yourself now might even remind you what matters while you're still here to live it.

## What to Include (The Nuts & Bolts)

Think of the obituary as the "official record." You can always spice it up, but the basics should be here:

- **Full Name** (and nicknames, if you want them used)

- **Dates** (birth and death)

- **Places** (where you were born, lived, and maybe where you died which someone else will add later, of course.)

- **Family** (spouse, children, grandchildren, parents, siblings—list who matters most)

- **Education/Work** (schools, career highlights, military service if relevant)

- **Clubs, Faith, Community** (church, volunteer work, groups)

- **Service Details** (funeral/memorial time, place, donation info instead of flowers)

## What Makes It Memorable (The Spark)

This is where you get to inject *you*.

- **Personality:** Were you funny? Quirky? Known for always bringing dessert? Say it.

- **Passions:** Hobbies, causes, and things that lit you up.

- **Stories:** Add a short anecdote—like the time you got lost in Paris or won a pie-eating contest.

- **Signature Line:** Something only you would say, or a motto you lived by.

## Biography Option

If "obituary" feels too stiff, write a short **life bio** instead—like the back of a book jacket about you. It doesn't need to be published in the paper; it can be something your family shares at your service, in a program, or on social media. This gives you way more freedom to highlight your adventures, relationships, and beliefs.

**Example to get you started:**
**Thomas "Tom" Reynolds** never met a weekend project he couldn't over complicate. Born and raised in Kansas, he built a life rooted in family, faith, and the kind of stubborn optimism that made him believe duct tape could fix almost anything...

## Real Life Stories

**The Straight-Laced Version** – Tom's kids stuck to just the basics: names, dates, job titles. People at his service said, "That didn't sound like the man we knew." The opportunity was lost.

**The Self-Written Bio** – Ed wrote his own a year before he passed. His daughter said, "It was like one last letter to all of us—funny, heartfelt, so very Dad."

- Lesson: details are fine, but voice is everything.

## Mini Homework Prompt:

Write a short draft of your obituary or bio. Don't overthink it—just start with these prompts:

- "What I hope people remember most about me is..."

_______________________________________________

_______________________________________________

_______________________________________________

- "One story I hope gets told at my funeral is..."

_______________________________________________

_______________________________________________

_______________________________________________

_______________________________________________

- "If my life had a headline, it would be…"

_______________________________________________

_______________________________________________

_______________________________________________

Write a paragraph or two, tuck it in with your other documents, and update it every couple of years.

> *Think of it as your last mic drop -don't let someone else write your final punch line.*

## 📝 Notes & Next Steps

Use this space to jot down ideas, phrases, or stories you want included in your obituary. Write what you'd want people to remember—your quirks, your proudest moments, your greatest loves, and even the funny mishaps that made you, *you.*

This chapter was about writing your own obituary—crafting the final story in your own voice instead of leaving it to someone else. Capture the essence of your life, the lessons you've learned, and the legacy you want to leave behind. Think of it as your last mic drop—make it honest, heartfelt, and a little bit unforgettable.

__________________________________

__________________________________

__________________________________

__________________________________

__________________________________

__________________________________

__________________________________

__________________________________

__________________________________

__________________________________

__________________________________

__________________________________

__________________________________

# CHAPTER 13

# FINAL PLANS: YOUR LAST (AFTER) PARTY

> *Everyone wants to go to heaven, but nobody wants to die to get there.*

## *(a.k.a. Don't Make Your Family Play Guessing Games With Your Corpse)*

Congratulations, planner — you've made it to the home stretch. Now it's time to decide how you want to bow out. Think of this as your ultimate RSVP: do you want a solemn funeral, a margarita-fueled bash, or to become a tree? (Yes, that's a thing.)

Here's the blunt truth: if you don't write this stuff down, your family will have to figure it out while they're grieving. And unlike guessing if you'd prefer spaghetti or tacos for dinner, this is heavier. Do they bury you? Cremate you? Scatter your ashes over the ocean or the 50-yard line? Or do they just argue in the funeral home parking lot until everyone is an emotional wreck?

You get to choose. (Otherwise, they'll be left with stress, guilt, and possibly a family feud that lasts longer than your service.

# The Menu of Options  (Because Death Isn't Just "Box or Urn" Anymore)

- **Traditional Burial** – Casket + cemetery plot.
  Pro: Familiar. Comforting ritual.
  Con: $8k–$12k average in the U.S. (that's a lot of dirt money).

- **Cremation (fire or water)** – You become ashes.
  Pro: Affordable ($1k–$3k). Flexible.
  Con: Still pay for box for the viewing.
  Some families really hate not having a gravesite to visit.

- **Green Burial** – Eco-friendly, biodegradable, no chemicals.
  Pro: Kind to the planet.
  Con: Not available everywhere.

- **Alkaline Hydrolysis (Water Cremation)** – Body dissolved with water + alkali.
  Pro: Low energy. "Gentle."
  Con: Not legal everywhere yet.

- **Body Donation** – Science gets your body. You get to keep teaching even after you're gone.
  Pro: Usually free. Legacy of giving. You can finally go to that medical university tuition free.
  Con: Not all programs accept everyone.

- **Cryonics** – Frozen in liquid nitrogen. Maybe revived someday.
  Pro: Theoretically, second chance at life.
  Con: Crazy expensive. Also, does it work?

- **Tree Pod Burial** – Body or ashes in a pod beneath a tree. You literally become nature.

Pro: Symbolic, eco-friendly, poetic.
Con: Not as "visit-able" as a traditional grave.

The right choice isn't about money or tradition. It's about what feels like you.

## Service Styles: The Vibe Check

- **Traditional Funeral:** Formal, religious/cultural, often with a casket.

- **Memorial / Celebration of Life:** Happens after burial or cremation. Can be anywhere—church, beach, brewery. Stories + memories.

- **Living Memorial:** Throw your own party while you're alive. (Yes, you can attend your own funeral. Champagne optional...often encouraged.)

## Informing Your Family

When it comes to funerals, planning is step one, but telling the family is step two. Write it down, tuck it in this kit, and tell at least one trusted person where to find it.

If you're brave, have the convo with your spouse, kids, or BFF. But if not, at least tell your executor or your "favorite child" (every family has one). Make sure they know:

- How you want your body handled (burial, cremation, donation, etc.)

- What type of service you want (funeral, celebration, living memorial)

- Who should be informed (and who should NOT—yes, you can blacklist people)

> Any special touches (songs, readings, locations, food, tequila shots, whatever feels right.)

## Real Life Stories: Done Right (and So Wrong)

### The Guessing Game

Brenda died without leaving instructions. Her three kids fought over burial vs. cremation vs. a beach party. The fight dragged on for weeks, the service was delayed, and the family was a mess.

### The After-Party Queen

Carmen left crystal-clear plans: cremation, ashes at sea, then a fiesta at her favorite Mexican restaurant with margaritas on her. Her family laughed through tears, celebrating her exactly the way she wanted.

### The Gift of Donation

Alan donated his body to a medical school. His family held a small memorial, later received his ashes, and felt proud knowing he was still teaching. His daughter said, "That was so Dad."

### Section Summary – Final Plans

- Pick your method: burial, cremation, donation, green burial, tree pod, or cryonics.

- Decide your service style: traditional, memorial, celebration, or living memorial.

- Write it down.

- Tell your family (at least one person + your executor).

- Cover details: who to notify, what vibe you want, how you want to be remembered.

- Write down how you want your body handled. (Burial, cremation, tree pod, etc.)

_______________________________________________

_______________________________________________

- Write down the type of service you'd want.

_______________________________________________

_______________________________________________

- Add one "signature touch" — a song, a food, a place. Think of it as your personal party favor.

_______________________________________________

_______________________________________________

- _"Write it down, or your send-off might look more like a committee meeting than a celebration of you."_

## Final Plans Worksheet

_(Capture Your Wishes for Funeral Memorial, and Beyond?_

### Section 1: Body Disposition Preferences

| | |
|---|---|
| Choice (Burial, Cremation, Groen Burial, Donation, Other) | |
| Preferred Location (Cemetery, Scattering Site, Tree Pod, etc.): | |

| Casket/Um/Container Preference | |
|---|---|
| Special Instructions (eco-friendly, religious nites, etc): | |

## Section 2: Service Preferences

| Service Type (Funeral Colebration of Life, Memorial, Living Memorial | |
|---|---|
| Service Location Church, Funeral Home. Outdoors Pub, etc) | |
| Open/Closed Casket (if applicable | |
| Officiant/Speaker Host | |
| Music/Songs Requested | |
| Readings/Poems/Scriptures | |
| Food/Drink/Recepton Details: | |
| Dress Code or Theme (formal, casual, colorful, etc) | |
| Other Special Touches (photos, videos, rhaals, etc.) | |

## Section 3: People to Notify

| Name | Relationship | Contact Info |
|---|---|---|
| | | |
| | | |
| | | |
| | | |
| | | |

| | | |
| --- | --- | --- |
| | | |
| | | |
| | | |

*Section 4: Additional Instructions or Notes*

| |
| --- |
| |
| |
| |
| |
| |
| |
| |
| |

Use this space to capture your choices, details, and any follow-up tasks from this chapter. Write down who needs to be contacted, what arrangements you've made, and any preferences for your service, burial, cremation, or donation. Add notes about songs, readings, or special touches that feel like you.

This chapter was about **your final plans—the how, where, and what of your last goodbye.** Whether you want a quiet ceremony or one hell of a celebration, document it clearly and share it with someone you trust. The goal: no guessing games, no family feuds—just a send-off that feels true to your story.

# CHAPTER 14

# LEGACY PLANNING: YOUR LETTERS & LASTING IMPACT

> *We all die. The goal isn't to live forever; it's to create something that will.*

## *(a.k.a. The Stuff That Actually Matters When the Wi-Fi's Off and You're Gone)*

Let's be real: the paperwork will get sorted out. Your bank accounts will be closed, your Facebook page might get turned into a "Remembering" profile, and your car will eventually find a new driveway. But your words? Your stories? The way you made people feel? That's the part no executor, probate judge, or financial advisor can duplicate.

The truth is, paperwork covers logistics. Legacy covers your soul.

I learned that the hard way. A few weeks after my husband died, I was sitting on the bathroom floor—red-eyed, snot-covered, surrounded by tissues and silence—when my 20-year-old daughter walked in. She sat beside me for a while, then quietly said, "Mom, death is hard, but life is harder." And she was right. Death was a thunderclap that shattered everything—but what came after was the real work. Learning how to breathe again. How to get up when the bed feels like an anchor. Learning how to face the quiet when every hour feels like swimming through Jello.

Grief rewires you. It rearranges everything you thought you knew about strength, love, and time. But it also reveals what truly lasts—the things that can't be lost in a move or divided in probate. A few years later, when my friend's husband died suddenly, I saw it all play out again. The panic. The confusion. The mountain of decisions no one wants to make when their heart's been ripped open. And I realized something so simple, it stopped me cold: planning your legacy isn't morbid. It's love in practical form. It's saying, "Here, I made this easier for you."

It's ensuring your family doesn't just inherit your bills, your sofa, or the half-used shampoo in the shower. They inherit your heart. Your laughter. The words only you could say.

Because when you're gone, what they'll need most isn't your stuff—it's your story.

## Why This Step Matters

By now, you've covered the boring-but-critical stuff — wills, debts, documents, passwords, even your after-party plans. Good job. But there's one thing all that can't do: it can't tell your people what they meant to you.

This step is about leaving *more than paperwork.* It's about saying the words you don't want to die with. The apologies you never made. The "I love you's" you thought they just "knew." The gratitude you always felt but never said out loud.

And this is not a surprise: people almost never regret oversharing their love. They regret staying quiet.

Legacy letters (or videos, journals, audio notes — whatever your style) are your mic drop. Your chance to be remembered not just for what you owned, but for who you were.

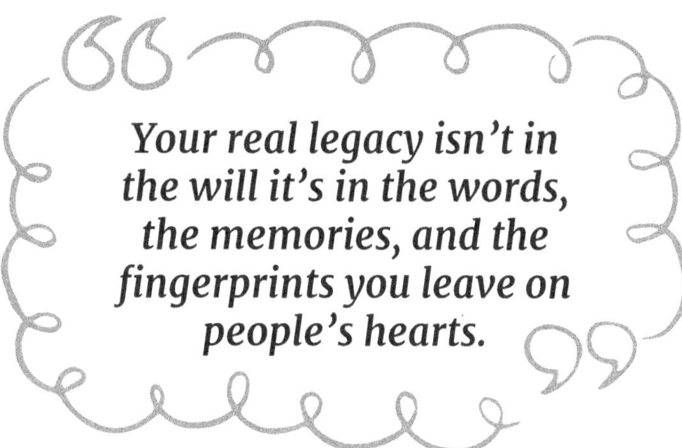


## What to Include in Your Legacy Letters

Think of this like building your own highlight reel — including  the cheesy music and slow-motion flashbacks. This isn't about being perfect; it's about being real. The moments, the people, the laughter, the lessons — all of it deserves a place in your story.

**Apologies & Forgiveness:**
Clear the air while you still can. Don't let grudges become family heirlooms. Whether it's something small you said in a moment of frustration or a deep hurt that's lingered for years, this is your chance to let it go. Sometimes forgiveness isn't about excusing what happened — it's about freeing everyone involved, including yourself. You don't have to tie every loose end into a bow; just soften what's hard before you go.

**Gratitude:**
Name names. Call out the people who shaped you — the friend who stood by you in your worst moments, the teacher who believed in you, the neighbor who shoveled your driveway without being asked. Gratitude doesn't

need to be flowery; it just needs to be honest. Let people know they mattered to you. The simplest thank-you can echo for generations.

**Love:**
Say it. Out loud. On paper. In every way you can. "I love you." "I'm proud of you." "You changed my life." Don't assume they already know. Love never gets old, and no one ever complains about hearing it too much. Pour it out freely — your words will become the thing they cling to when the world feels too quiet.

**Stories & Memories:**
Tell the stories that define you — the ones that make people laugh, roll their eyes, or cry. The time you got lost on vacation and found your favorite spot by accident. The recipe you always burned but made anyway. The ridiculous holiday mishap everyone still talks about. These aren't just anecdotes; they're the breadcrumbs of who you were. Long after your things are gone, these stories will keep you alive in the best way possible.

**Goodbye:**
Skip the Hallmark script and make it human. Be truthful. Be funny, if that's who you are. Be gentle, if that's how you lived. A goodbye isn't the end — it's your closing note, your final imprint. It's not about perfect words; it's about saying, *"This was me. And I loved you the best I could."*

# Real Life Stories: Words That Outlived the Body

### The Regret
Paul never told his kids he was proud of them. Ever. When he died, his silence cut deeper than the funeral. That's what they remembered most — *what he didn't say.*

## The Letters

Janet wrote one for each of her children. Each included a memory, advice, and love. Today, those letters are their most treasured inheritance — worth more than money or heirlooms.

## The Videos

Marcus recorded short clips during cancer treatment. His family plays them on birthdays and anniversaries. His daughter said, "It's like he's still cheering us on."

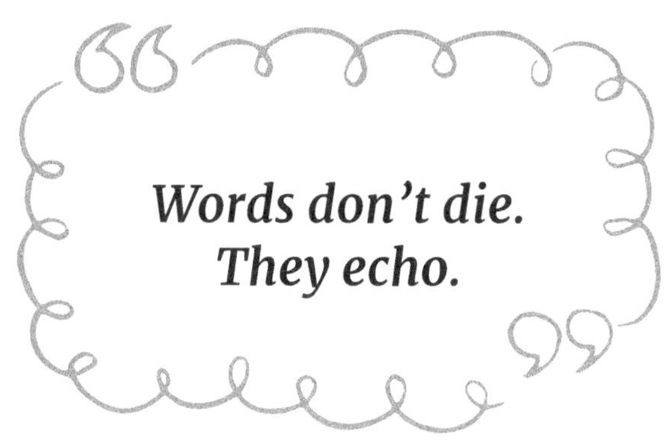


## Mini Homework Prompt:

Pick one person. Write them a note today. Doesn't have to be long. Doesn't have to be perfect. Just honest. Use one of these as your starter:

- "I'm sorry for..."

- "Thank you for..."

- "One of my favorite memories with you is..."

- "I love you because..."

Done. That's legacy.

Use this space to jot down ideas, names, and heartfelt messages that came to mind in this chapter. Write who you want to leave letters for, what memories or lessons you want to share, and any meaningful gestures or "acts of love" you still want to do.

This chapter was about **legacy planning—writing the words and creating the moments that will outlive you.** Your letters, videos, and small acts of kindness are the fingerprints you leave on the hearts of others. Start writing, start sharing, and let your love echo long after you're gone.

# CHAPTER 15

# MARK YOUR MEMORIES: KEEPING YOUR STORY ALIVE

> *Memories are the best souvenirs of life.*

## *(a.k.a. More Laughs, Less Clutter)*

Not to be cold, but most of the stuff you leave behind won't matter. Your couch will end up on Facebook Marketplace. Your car will get traded in for something that doesn't smell like stale fries. And that house you obsessed over? Eventually, some couple will knock down walls and ask, "Who painted this room blue on purpose?"

But your memories—that's the real inheritance. Nobody gets sentimental over a chipped mug or the world's heaviest coffee table. But they'll remember your laugh. The way you butchered song lyrics in the car. How you burned breakfast every Sunday but called it "family tradition." That's what sticks.

People won't remember how your furniture was arranged; they'll remember what it felt like to be around you. The running jokes, the stories, the one-liners that somehow became family legend. That's the stuff that lasts—because it's not about the things you owned, it's about the life you actually lived.

## Why Memories > Stuff

When people talk about loved ones, they don't say:

- "Wow, her 401(k) balance was breathtaking."

- "I'll never forget Dad's impeccable ability to pay his bills on time."

**Nope. They remember:**

- The way Dad whistled in the garage like he was auditioning for a bird choir.

- The way Mom could make grown men cry by raising one eyebrow expressing her extreme disapproval.

- The chaos of family road trips when the cartop carrier was torn off in the parking garage.

- The Sunday dinners where laughter was louder than the Super Bowl.

Stuff fades. Stories endure. And if you don't capture them, they die with you.

## How to Capture the Good Stuff

- **Photo Collections:** Organize them, label them. Otherwise, in 30 years your grandkids will ask, "Who's the guy with the creepy mustache?" and nobody will know.

- **Journals or Letters:** Write down the stories, the lessons, the "don't do what I did" moments. Don't worry about grammar. This isn't for your English teacher.

- **Video or Audio Recordings:** Record yourself telling a story, cracking up, or giving life advice. (Pro tip: your real laugh is worth more than your real estate.)

- **Recipes & Traditions:** Don't let Grandma's secret pie crust recipe die with her. Write it down. Or better yet, teach it with all the "oops" moments included.

- **Heirloom Tags:** Stick notes on things. "This fishing pole caught exactly one fish and 2 beer cans." Suddenly, junk becomes treasure.

- **Memory Boxes:** Ticket stubs, love notes, old Polaroids, that keychain from your first car. Box it up. It's basically your personal time capsule.

## Real Life Stories: The Good, The Quirky, The Tearjerkers

### The Recipe Binder

After Nina passed, her family found a binder full of her recipes with snarky notes like, "Don't burn this like I did in '92." Now they cook from it every holiday — it's like she's still roasting them from beyond.

### The Audio Tape

Sam's grandfather recorded cassettes in the '80s, rambling about life during the war. Decades later, his great-grandkids still play them. "It's like we actually know him," one said.

### The Forgotten Box

Lisa found a shoebox after her dad died, stuffed with letters and postcards he never mentioned. She said, "It was like meeting a younger, weirder version of my dad."

Moral of the story: Don't let people piece your life together from random scraps. Leave it intentionally.

△ Pick one memory to capture this week — write it, record it, or snap it.

△ Choose one item you own with a story. Write a note about it and attach it.

△ Bonus: Start a "Memory Box" or digital folder. Every time you think, "Oh, that's a good story," drop it in. Future-you (and future-them) will thank you.

> *Memories are the most valuable inheritance -label them before they turn into family mysteries.*

## Memory Work

### Section 1: Life Stories
(Capture stories, lessons, and traditions that matter)

My favorite memory:______________________________

___________________________________________

___________________________________________

A time I felt truly proud:_________________________

___________________________________________

___________________________________________

184

My biggest adventure:_______________________________

_______________________________________________________

_______________________________________________________

Something I learned the hard way:_______________________

_______________________________________________________

_______________________________________________________

A moment that changed my life:_________________________

_______________________________________________________

_______________________________________________________

## *Section 2: Family and Traditions*

My favorite holiday and moments:_______________________

_______________________________________________________

_______________________________________________________

The best meal I ever ate/cooked:_______________________

_______________________________________________________

_______________________________________________________

A recipe I want passed down:____________________________

_______________________________________________________

_______________________________________________________

Our funniest family tradition:__________________________

_______________________________________________________

_______________________________________________________

Something unique about our family:________________________

__________________________________________________

## *Section 3 Lessons and Advice:*

One piece of advice for future generations:

__________________________________________________

__________________________________________________

Something I wish I'd done differently:     _________________

__________________________________________________

__________________________________________________

The best decision I ever made:     _____________________

__________________________________________________

__________________________________________________

What I want you to remember me for:     _________________

__________________________________________________

__________________________________________________

Use this space to record the stories, photos, or memories you want to preserve. Write down where your photos are stored, which traditions or recipes you want passed down, and any items that hold special meaning.

This chapter was about marking your memories and keeping your story alive. Capture the laughter, the lessons, and the little things that made your life uniquely yours. Label the photos, record the stories, and make sure the people you love can keep reliving the moments that mattered most.

# CHAPTER 16

# YOUR DREAMS ✦

> *Dreams are the whispers of the soul, asking to be spoken out loud.*

## *(a.k.a. The Stuff That Outlives You — Without the Paperwork)*

Alright, deep breath. This is the last chapter — and guess what? No forms, no signatures, no notarized anything. This one isn't about paperwork. It's about heart work.

You've done the heavy lifting already: wills, directives, passwords, funeral playlists (yes, including that song everyone begs you to shut off.) But this? This is where you leave the good stuff — your dreams.

Because here's the truth: life is noisy. Between paying bills, dragging yourself through workweeks, raising kids, and wondering why laundry multiplies like rabbits, your soul-level conversations tend to get buried. The "What do I want for you?" and "What do I hope you never forget?" talks rarely make it to the dinner table.

This chapter is your chance to bring them back up. Think of it as planting seeds for tomorrow.

# Dreams as a Gift

I was lucky enough to have a random, soul-deep conversation with my husband about his dreams for our kids just minutes before he died. It was a gift wrapped in the simplest words— one I was able to pass down to our children when he was gone. And I can't begin to tell you how those dreams still steer them years later.

That's the magic here: dreams outlive you. They ripple forward, shaping the choices of the people you love. They can be a compass in the middle of someone's storm, a flashlight when they're lost, or a swift kick in the pants when they're stalling.

What Dreams Might You Share?

- **Wisdom:** The stuff you learned the hard way so they don't have to. ("Don't date someone who thinks gaslighting is a personality trait.")

- **Encouragement:** The reminders they'll need when they want to give up. ("Say yes to the trip. Apply for the job. Always order dessert.")

- **Vision:** The hopes you have for their future — not to control them, but to remind them how much possibility their life holds.

- **Gratitude:** The quiet reflections of what mattered most to you — the people, the love, the laughter. Gratitude makes the sharp edges of life a little softer.

# The Power of Words for Tomorrow

Here's the thing: your words can outlast you in ways you can't imagine. One sentence in a letter might be the reason someone finally takes the leap, forgives themselves, or finally follows their passion. You may never know it, but your words could be the spark that pulls someone out of a dark season, or the steady voice they hear when they're lost and wondering what to do next.

Your dreams—the ones you dared to say out loud—might become someone else's permission slip to stop waiting for "someday." Maybe your daughter will finally take that solo trip you always talked about. Maybe your best friend will start that business you once dreamed of building together. Maybe your words will remind someone that it's okay to start over at any age, to love again, to live louder.

And if there's one thing this whole book has taught you, it's that "someday" is a terrible plan. Life doesn't wait for the perfect timing, the right savings account, or the courage to magically appear. It happens in the messy middle, between the plans and the pauses. So write it down. Say the thing. Leave the words that prove you lived boldy—and that it mattered.

## Real Life Stories: Dreams That Linger

### A Father's Promise

When Ethan passed, he left each of his kids a letter ending with: *"Never live small. Take the trip. Love big. Don't be afraid to fall flat on your face — it just means you tried."* His daughter says she rereads those words before every big decision.

### A Grandmother's Hopes

Rose wrote: *"I hope you dance. I hope you sing loud, even off-key. I hope you find love that feels like home."* Her grandkids still repeat her words to each other like a family mantra.

Dreams don't die. They become someone else's story.

## Section Summary – Your Dreams

- Write a personal letter sharing your dreams for the future.

- Reflect on wisdom, lessons, and even your epic mistakes.

- Share hopes for your kids, grandkids, or favorite humans.

- Encourage them to take risks and live big.

- Root it all in gratitude — because gratitude is the classiest final act  you can leave behind.

## Mini Homework Prompt:

Take one quiet moment this week. Write down a dream you hold for someone you love — a child, a partner, a friend. Don't edit it. Don't dress it up. Just write it, stick it in an envelope with their name, and tuck it away. Whether they read it tomorrow or twenty years from now, it will hit them right in the heart.

Use this space to write down the dreams, wishes, and hopes you want to pass on. Jot down who you want to share them with, what you still want to say, and the messages you hope will guide the people you love long after you're gone.

This chapter was about **sharing your dreams—the ones that outlive you and inspire others to keep going.** Write the words that light the way: your wisdom, your encouragement, your vision for their future. Because when you share your dreams, you give permission for theirs to grow.

# Closing

## THE FINAL LOVE LETTER

And now, here you are — the end of the book, but not the end of your story. You've faced the hard questions, made the plans, gathered the papers, and left your footprints of love and intention behind. But before you close this chapter, there is one last gift you can give.

Write a love letter to yourself.

Not to your children, not to your partner, not to your friends. To you. To the one who carried this life — in joy, in sorrow, in mess and in beauty. Because this was your story, and it deserves to be remembered in your own words.

Tell the truth of what it felt like to be you. Remember the moments that shaped you — the first time you looked into your child's eyes, the dizzy happiness, the terror, the awe. Recall the heartbreaks too — losing a parent, saying goodbye to a spouse, carrying grief like an invisible weight. Tell  of the way your life shifted with the decades: the fire of your twenties, the stretching of your thirties, the deepening wisdom of later years.

Name what you will miss. The cool grass beneath your feet. The sting of a brain freeze from eating ice cream too fast. The first sip of your favorite wine, shared with someone you loved. The way your grandchild's chubby fingers wrapped around yours as you walked together, time slowing down for just a moment.

And allow yourself to wonder. What do you believe now about heaven, or what comes after? Does it feel nearer than it once did? More possible? Less distant? Let those questions live here too — unanswered maybe, but wholly yours.

If writing feels too heavy, speak it aloud. Record it. Ask a friend or family member to capture it for you. But leave it somewhere. Leave it as a final testimony that you were here, and that you loved being you.

Because one day, when someone asks, *"What was it like to be you?"* — this letter will answer. And it will echo with gratitude, tenderness, and truth.

This is your last chapter. Your final bow. Not just the life you leave behind, but the love you carried through it.

# Epilogue

So that's it. You've done the work most people spend their whole lives avoiding. You've organized the papers, made the plans, even written the words that will outlive you. Now? You get to live lighter. You get to laugh at the little things again — the ice cream brain freezes, the late-night phone calls that always go too long.

This book was never really about death. It was about life — about making space for you to spend your days with less worry and the people you love to grieve with more peace. So take a deep breath. Enjoy your coffee a little slower. Hug your people a little tighter. Smile at the fact that, after all the talk, you finally got your shit together.

# Resources

Because let's be honest: Sometimes you need more than a pep talk in life. You need the actual links, numbers, and places to go when it's time to get the paperwork done. Here are some trusted spots that might help along the way.

**End-of-Life Planning & Legal Documents**
**Advance Directives by State – CaringInfo.org:** caringinfo.org (free, state-specific forms you can download)

**National Hospice and Palliative Care Organization:** nhpco.org (resources on living wills, care planning, and palliative options)

**IRS – Filing Final Returns & Estate Taxes:** irs.gov/individuals/deceased-taxpayers (executor guidance, final 1040s, and estate obligations)

- **Tax Foundation – State Estate & Inheritance Taxes:** tax foundation.org (clear breakdown of which states levy extra taxes after death)

**Caregiving & Long-Term Care**

- **Eldercare Locator (Administration for Community Living):** eldercare.acl.gov (connects you to caregiving, housing, and aging resources near you)

- **AARP Long-Term Care Cost Calculator:** aarp.org/longtermcarecosts (estimates care costs by state and city)

**Family Caregiver Alliance:** caregiver.org (practical support, education, and legal/financial tools for caregivers)

## Downsizing & Housing Options

△ **National Council on Aging – Downsizing & Housing Resources:** ncoa.org (guides on simplifying your home, housing choices, and aging well)

△ **55places.com:** 55places.com (directory of 55+ and active adult communities nationwide)

## Gifting & Charitable Giving

△ **National Philanthropic Trust:** nptrust.org (overview of donor-advised funds, family giving, and charitable strategies)

△ **Charity Navigator:** charitynavigator.org (evaluate charities before you give)

## Digital Estate & Password Management

△ **Password Managers:** 1password.com, lastpass.com, bitwarden.com

△ **Google Inactive Account Manager:** support.google.com/accounts (set what happens to your Google account after death)

**Facebook Legacy Contact:** facebook.com/help (appoint someone to manage or close your account after you're gone)

## Obituary, Biography & Memories

△ **StoryWorth:** storyworth.com (weekly prompts that become a bound keepsake book of your life stories)

△ **FamilySearch Memories:** familysearch.org (free tool for uploading and sharing photos, documents, and stories)

△ **MayoClinic.org:** Creating Living Wills and Advanced Directives for Medical Decisions

Thanks for being here — really here —
for the conversations most people avoid.

If it made you think, laugh,
or get your shit together even a little,
that's enough.

Take care of your people.
Take care of yourself.

With heart,
— Shelli